CHOOSING ME

Dear Becca,

Keep choosing you!

Love, Kelly

GW00644846

MOONSHOT PUBLISHING

www.moonshot-publishing.com

Moonshot Publishing B.V. at Laren, The Netherlands

2024 Moonshot Publishing B.V.

Text by Kelly Weekers ©

Final editing by David Reiss and Annoesjka Oostindiër

and Design by Coco Bookmedia

ISBN 9789083341798

For information: Moonshot Publishing, Oosterend 13, 1251 HM Laren, The Netherlands. Registered with the Netherlands Chamber of Commerce under number 85922145.

Books in the Moonshot Publishing catalog may be purchased for educational or commercial use or for sales promotions. For more information, please email: support@moonshot-publishing.com.

Visit us online at moonshot-publishing.com.

The most beautiful
thing you can become is yourself.
Welcome home.

TABLE OF CONTENTS

INTRODUCTION

Ever wondered what people regret the most when they are nearing the end of their lives? Not having lived their lives the way they wanted, but according to the expectations of others. Australian palliative nurse Bronnie Ware counsels people on their deathbeds and wrote about these regrets in her book "*The Top Five Regrets of the Dying.*" All too often people don't think about what they really wanted to do with their lives until they realize the end is near. Only when it's too late do most people start to think, "Shit, if only I had worked a little less hard, if only I had the courage to express my feelings, if only I had stayed in touch with friends, if only I had allowed myself more happiness." If only, if only, if only. At the end of our lives, all kinds of unfulfilled wishes suddenly become obvious. In her book, Bronnie Ware shows that when the end is near, almost everyone had the same realization: if only I had been true to myself and lived my life in a way that made me happy.

It is not only on our deathbed that feelings of regret about the choices we made, or *didn't* make, surface. Many of us also experience this frustration during the rush hour of our lives, especially when we are in the phase where we must achieve different goals and fill many different roles, from child, colleague and partner to parent and friend, with all the expectations and opinions that go with them. Especially during these times it can be hard not to lose track of who we really are. And it can be difficult to stay true to yourself because you keep getting distracted by how you want to be or think you should be and by all the labels that other people put on you. If I had to list reasons why people choose to see a psychologist, number one would be: I don't feel like myself anymore. I can't really be who I am and I'm not doing what makes me happy. People experience all kinds of symptoms, from stress and anxiety to panic and depression. Often what is behind their request for help is this feeling of not knowing who they are or not daring to live the way they want. Whether you go to a psychologist or a coach, do some soul searching, or spend an evening philosophizing with a friend at the kitchen table, for most of us that stress, that feeling of lacking control and of being out of balance, is the reason that at some point we all ask ourselves the question: "but what do I really want?" And that question is often what's needed to kickstart change. That change may involve who we love, our careers, where we live or the people we spend time with. It is the moment you realize that for you to be happy you have to make yourself a priority. That you have to truly choose yourself.

"I choose myself." That statement triggers a strong reaction in many people. It leads to comments like "oh, I'd also like that, I don't even know what makes me happy anymore," but also remarks like "wow, how selfish, you're not the only person in the world. Don't you care about other people?" The association with selfishness is especially persistent. But choosing yourself is not about *not* choosing others. Of course, you can be there for your family, for your friends and for people you don't know, but who desperately need your help. What "I choose myself" means to me is this: I am my own best friend. I am worthy of being loved and the first person who is going to give me unconditional love is myself. I take full responsibility for my life. I am in control of my thoughts, feelings, and actions. I value myself and I dare to say no and to set boundaries. I listen to my own inner voice; I am aware of what I need, and I believe that I am the one who can give it to me. For me, choosing myself means that if I take good care of myself, I can also take good care of others.

Really knowing, being and choosing yourself has a tremendous, positive transformative effect on yourself, others and your life. But it is also a challenge, because knowing and being yourself can be pretty damn difficult. Arranging your life in a way that suits you best, in balance with the things that must happen and with an eye for the people who are important to you, is something we can struggle with for a lifetime. It's a bit like putting together an IKEA closet. When you start it all looks quite simple. You might think "I'll have it done in the blink of an eye." It's easy to say "you just have to stay true to yourself" – but when you find yourself juggling all the screws and bolts of the KNERPSTA, that feeling of healthy enthusiasm quickly turns into sweating, frustration, blind panic and a minor mental breakdown. And if you think the closet was complicated, it's easy-peasy compared to you. You were delivered without step-by-step instructions and chances are you're missing some screws and bolts too. That's exactly why I think it's time to teach you how to write and read your own manual. And to give you some tips about the parts you might still be missing and need to add, so that you can also build a sturdy structure for yourself.

At some point, we all think about the direction we want our lives to take. Our desires change over the years, and that requires some regular adjustments in how you see yourself and how you want to shape your life. This book lets you take an honest look at yourself and your life. Maybe it confirms that you already have a very good idea of who you are and that you are doing a pretty good job of staying true to yourself. Maybe it's a wake-up call that you still have a lot of work to do. In any case, this book will make you aware that you may, no, *must* put yourself first and will give you a plan for how to do it. This book will give you insights, tools, and assignments – feel free to grab a pen and paper – to help you know yourself better. And once you know yourself, you will make choices that are in line with your happiness, and you can start living accordingly *today*. So that on your deathbed, when you are asked what you regret, you can say, "Regret? I don't have regrets. I dared to live life the way I wanted. I have always been true to myself, and I have been there for, and enjoyed myself with, the people I care about. I chose myself and that is the best choice I ever made. I'm happy."

- Kelly

KNOWING YOURSELF

Do you know who you
are if you don't let others
tell you who to be?

YOUR PAST

D on't worry, this is not the part where I say "lie down on my couch so we can pick apart your past." The fact is you will never be free of the past if you keep focusing on it. Constantly looking backwards and dwelling on all the misery that has happened to you will get you nowhere. The past is a part of your life that you can no longer change and that you simply cannot influence. My goal is not to endlessly analyze and risk getting bogged down in old stories, but purely to see which pieces of the puzzle from your past you need to understand yourself better. If you understand what influence your past has had, and still has, on how you think, feel and behave today, then you can let go of those parts that no longer help you and that keep you from being who you are and want to be. So that you can live your life the way that you want.

Maybe at this moment you don't know who you are, what you like and what direction you want your life to take. Maybe you know what you do *not* want. Or maybe you've reached a point in your life where you've got it pretty much figured out but you want to put all your ducks in a row. Maybe you keep falling into the trap of pleasing others. Daring to put yourself first would bring you so much peace, but guilt prevents you from doing things differently. Maybe you feel you have to make choices, but you just don't know which one is right, because you are so influenced by the voices of others. Maybe you don't know if you should listen to your head or your heart – and all these doubts stop you before you can make a decision. Whether it's small wishes or big dreams and changes, the only way out is in. Inward, to be precise. You won't find the answers by looking around you, but by looking at yourself in the mirror. So the past is a very important factor. It's not about blaming the people who played a big part in it or looking at what went wrong and where you might have made mistakes yourself, but about knowing how to break certain old patterns and make the choices that are best for you right now.

In the context of self-development, you can talk endlessly about the past. About different attachment styles, complexes, family dynamics, traumas, triggers, defense mechanisms, coping styles, parenting styles and so much more. What I want to achieve with this book is to help you get to know yourself and learn how to make better choices for yourself. So, I will only delve into those aspects of your past that I believe will help you achieve this in the easiest way possible. What I don't want to do is overwhelm you with information that makes you think, "never mind, this is too boring and complicated, whatever." If you want to dive deeper into your past, because it interests you or because it suits your growth process, then I certainly encourage that. There are lots of great books, trainings, mentors and coaching methods that can help you with this. But personally, I believe that we don't always have to make it very difficult for major change to happen. The trick is to keep it simple and practical, so that it's easy to understand and apply in daily life. Our lives are busy enough already! And of course so that "working on yourself" is not a slog, but actually a lot of fun! That's why I want to talk about trauma and conditions of worth. Simply put: what have you experienced in your life that has shaped you and when do you feel worthy of love and recognition? These past experiences form two important pillars that often make it difficult for us to choose ourselves.

In our youth we are programmed to think in certain ways. No one comes out unscathed. All of us carry stuff in our backpacks. Those things can be valuable, beautiful and helpful, but also sad, painful, traumatizing and everything in between. You watch and listen to your parents. You interact with your surroundings and mimic what you learn. You receive encouragement and disapproval. You experience things that impact you. All of this shapes you. If you don't watch out and keep lugging things around

You can only stop
repeating your past if you
understand your past.

in that backpack without occasionally throwing something out, it starts to become too heavy to carry. Especially if you plan on walking around with it for about eighty years. Why not take the bag off your back, turn it upside down and give it a good shake so that everything falls out? And then take a look at what's there. Maybe you didn't even realize half of the things you were carrying. You'll suddenly find something and think, "hey, that's handy, I can use that." And maybe there are also items in there where you think, "this isn't mine, it's my mother's." Or "this is mine, but I don't need it anymore." Then it's time to throw that junk out or give it back to the people it belonged to. And it doesn't have to be empty either! Carrying a well-filled backpack is not a bad thing. It helps you cope with life's challenges because you have some tools with you. But you don't have to be prepared for absolutely *everything*. If you go hiking in the woods for a few days, it's useful to bring some food, a gas stove to cook with and to know how it all works. It makes less sense to carry around an entire barbecue grill. It serves no purpose. At least, not anymore. That was handy when you were throwing a big party. Now it mainly gives you sore arms and legs. And maybe you can also leave the dartboard, lawn mower and inflatable pool at home.

What is in that backpack now, what can we still use and what should we throw out? To answer this important question, ask yourself: what comes to mind right away when I think about my past? What are the events or feelings – whether it's your upbringing, adolescent years, or adulthood – that I want to cherish? And what are the things that have really affected me in a negative way? What positive and negative experiences stand out immediately? The things in your backpack that you can name instantly, positive or negative, those are the things you are aware of. That's a great start because you can't change what you're not aware of. Later in the book, we'll see if maybe something else falls out of a side pocket that you didn't even know you had.

When we discuss negative experiences in the context of psychology, we pretty much always talk about trauma. Trauma is an emotional reaction to an impactful event you were exposed to or experienced. When we talk about trauma, it can mean different things for different people. As I said, no one comes out of life unscathed; life *is* experiences and subsequent growth. I have yet to meet a person who has not experienced trauma somewhere along the line. Trauma comes in all shapes and sizes. For some, it's a bruise that may feel a little sore when you press on it; for others, it's a near-death experience that immediately produces intense emotions of fear, sadness, shame, anger, or guilt. There are traumas where we think "yes, it must be terrible to go through something like that" but the person themself isn't too bothered by it, and then there are traumas that might seem small at first glance, but require years of therapy to work through. Trauma is very personal. In the context of getting to know yourself, it is always important to remember the following: there is no *one size fits all* way of dealing with things. Your feelings are *always* valid. If you struggled with something in your past, it is not up to anyone else to tell you how to feel about it. It just *is*. You can't argue about feelings, they are there. And they are independent of what someone else has gone through and how that person has experienced it. It's not a contest! Don't let anyone tell you that you're weak because of how you feel about something that happened to you. Or that you have not really dealt with what happened because you moved past it fairly easily. Everyone has their own way. The trick is to find your way.

Why is it so important to see and acknowledge trauma? Because as long as you are not in control of your trauma, it is in control of you, whether or not you are conscious of that fact. Trauma holds you captive and prevents you from truly being yourself. I cannot give you trauma therapy in this book. That goes much deeper. Therapy can help. If you feel overwhelmed by your emotions, I'd advise you to seek professional help. And please know that it's possible to achieve great results in a very short time.

However, there are things you can do for yourself. First, understand exactly how trauma affects you. Trauma causes you to hide a part of yourself. You did this to survive a stressful situation or period of time when you were younger. It was a strategy that helped you then, but often causes problems in the present. It stops you from doing what you really want to do and from being who you really want to be. Trauma distorts our thoughts, our emotions and our behavior. And to break free from that, it's important to thank that piece of yourself for keeping you safe all this time. Maybe your trauma caused you to shy away from things for a long time, maybe you didn't let people in, didn't dare to get attached or didn't dare to trust yourself. Be thankful that you were able to protect yourself that way. But also tell yourself that now is the time to find new ways that are more in line with who you really are.

One of the most powerful exercises for processing impactful events is to pay attention to your inner child. You can do this by closing your eyes and going back to your childhood. Now visualize yourself as a child sitting in your bedroom, or at the kitchen table or somewhere else where you often used to sit alone. Now picture your adult-self walking into that room and sitting down with yourself. I want you to visualize giving this younger version of yourself what you needed in that moment. Maybe that little boy or girl needs words of support, a hug, or a listening ear? Maybe you have a good cry together? You are that child. And you are also an adult who is now so much wiser and stronger and can look at situations differently. Intuitively give yourself everything you needed in that moment but didn't get. Give yourself the adult you needed.

No matter how old you are, there is still a small child inside you that deserves your attention. A child that wants to be acknowledged, loved and reassured. It's something a level-headed person might scoff at, "what nonsense," but let this book be exactly the tool you need to put you in touch with things you don't know about yet, but that may really work for you. Going back to difficult moments in your life can help you better understand why you're sensitive about things today. Once you see the child in yourself that needs attention, you can also become the adult you want to be. Does this exercise bring out a powerful response in you? Then we've found a bruise or trauma of yours. Or, at the end of the day, as I'm not one for labeling everything, just something that you should pay attention to. You might ask yourself: do I want to do something with what I've learned? In what way is this impacting me today? How does this affect how I feel and behave, how I engage in or maintain relationships? If there is something I have taken from my studies in psychology, it is to never take things for granted, but to always keep asking questions. Why is this the way it is? Why am I doing this this way? Maybe your trauma is that you often used to feel criticized. When you do the exercise, you may think back to a moment when you were sitting in your room, feeling sad because you heard for the umpteenth time that you will never be able to do what your sister or brother can do. That you are clumsy, not smart enough, too shy, or lazy. Realize that it's not strange that when you are criticized today, you immediately feel attacked. That you have trouble allowing people into your life and trusting them. By acknowledging that little boy or girl's feelings and giving that hug or reaching out more often when that feeling comes up today, you're going to find that your emotional reaction in the present will also fade into the background. In this way, you can help yourself repair past damage. Again, if bigger issues come up that really need further attention, I definitely recommend seeking out the help of a mental health professional. I share this exercise because I believe we can often help ourselves in the way a professional would, at least to a great extent. And with patience, love, and attention we can heal ourselves. In the end, you know yourself best.

Another thing we carry with us from our past, especially our upbringing and our early years, are our *conditions of worth*. Carl Rogers, a leading psychologist who was one of the first to believe in the human ability to develop and evolve throughout life, developed a theory that gives us insight into an important pattern in our personalities. In an ideal world, we would all receive unconditional love as children. Whoever you are, whatever you do, I love you, I see you, I am here for you. Unfortunately, the opposite is true. As children many of us were surrounded by conditional love. Often you received love, or not, when you did something well or not well according to the vision of the authority figures in your life, such as your parents. This teaches us to not really be ourselves, but to act like the person we need to be to receive that love. You learned as a child to fulfill certain conditions to be seen and loved by the important people in your life. Some examples of conditions of worth are: if I want to be of value, I must work hard. If I want to be of value, I must not cry. If I want to be of value, I must listen. If I want to be of value, I must have certain beliefs and only love people of a certain gender. These assumptions arise because you were praised or punished for showing that part of yourself. If you got good grades in school your parents were proud. If you got a lower grade, they were disappointed. If you raised your voice you were put in your place. If you were quiet, they told you how good you were. If you cried you heard "stop crying, it's not that bad," and if you kept your emotions bottled up you heard "oh my, you are so tough." All these voices shaped your character according to what the authority figures in your life valued. That was how you felt accepted. And that makes you hide the pieces of yourself that might receive disapproval and show only what you think will get approval. Only when you behave, think and feel a certain way are you worthy. And those conditions are often the strongest motivation behind our thoughts, feelings, and actions today.

Without getting too deep into the subject, it is good to think for yourself: what are my conditions of worth? What have I learned? What was I praised for? What was I rejected for? How does that impact my personality today? Am I still living according to those conditions? To figure this out, it is helpful to fill in the following sentence: If I want to be of value then I need to… What do you need to do? Think about it, but don't overthink it either. What is the first thing that comes to mind? If I want to be of value, then I must… Many people say things like obey, work hard, don't cry, don't get angry, be the best. Recognize what these sensitive areas are for you. If you don't know what your programming is, you will keep acting on these conditions all the time, even when they no longer fit with the person you want to be. Maybe they also cause unnecessary friction with your environment. Why exactly are you working so hard? Does that really make you happy? Or do you feel like a loser if you don't, because that was the signal you got when you were young? We look for our values in everything; from our work to our love life and friendships. But if they are not helpful values, they can also get you into a lot of trouble.

Think like your own coach more often. Be your own guru more often. Challenge yourself to question your perceptions and motivations. Is it so selfish to put myself first or is that just what I was taught as a child, and I don't really think that anymore? Am I lazy when I'm tired and get my rest or is that something I need and is there more to life than always being a top performer? Am I wrong if I want to start a romantic relationship with someone of the same gender or do others make me feel that way with their disapproving voices and looks, when I actually see things differently? The trick is to ask yourself better questions so that you get better answers. Is what I am thinking right now correct? Is what I am feeling correct? Is what I am doing right? Is this what I want and how I see myself or is this a voice from the past that no longer serves a purpose? Am I handling this situation this way because of what I experienced and learned as a child or are there other ways to look at it? Can I also feel a different way about this situation? Is there something else I can do right now that better fits who I am? Be open to new perspectives and make sure you have your best interests at heart in everything you do. As I said, we don't look at the past to assign blame, but to learn from it. Have you been given conditional love? Now give it to yourself unconditionally. Create your own values based on what you care about in this life. Allow yourself to be who you are and not who you think you should be according to the wishes or expectations of others.

So, we've talked about trauma and conditions of worth. Not the easiest subjects to start with. So why did I want to share this with you anyway? The art of analyzing your past is about discovering exactly why you feel a certain way and what limiting beliefs about yourself, others and life you have acquired. This allows you to rewrite them, so they no longer hold you back. An example. You may have a feeling of being excluded. Maybe that is objectively true, maybe that is a train of thought that recurs over and over in your life. When did you first feel excluded? When did you first feel less than others? When did you delude yourself that others could make better decisions for you? When did you first settle for an unhealthy relationship? When did you learn that it is normal for someone to manipulate you? Who instilled the belief that you can't achieve more than what you have achieved now, that you should be grateful for what you have and, above all, not want more? If you know who gave you those ideas and why, where exactly those traumas or conditions came from, then you can defuse them and develop your own ideas about yourself and the world around you. At least, if you are in fact tired of those previous ideas and beliefs because they don't fit you. Keep what you want to keep, discard what you no longer need, and dare to reinvent yourself.

Look at it this way; in the past we almost all believed in Santa Claus. That a man with a white beard rode across the roof on a sled pulled by flying reindeer made complete sense to us as children, but one day you wised up and left that fable behind. However, Santa Claus is not the only nonsense you have believed in. There are many more things that you have consciously and unconsciously picked up about life and about yourself that you are still swallowing, even though they don't make sense or no longer help you. Time to pop that bubble too. Cherish everything from your past that makes your life better. If there are parts of your past that only make life harder, let them go. Remember that your parents, caretakers, or environment usually did not have bad intentions in coloring your person and your reality. Usually, they simply acted out of love, or the desire to protect you, and the filter through which they also looked back at their own past. So, it was not always about bad intentions. It's just that they didn't always give you what you needed. They did their best according to what they knew. You can continue to live that way, or you can forge your own path. And the bright side

I embrace what's
behind me. I am grateful for where
I am now. I'm excited about
where I'm going.

of all this: every challenge you've had has helped you develop positive things that you wouldn't have learned about if you hadn't had this shit to deal with! If your parents were unpredictable in their behavior, you learned to tiptoe as a child. But you also learned to read people very well. Little traits, like the way someone says something, or their body language, it may not mean anything to someone who didn't have your childhood, but you can tell all sorts of things from it. How someone feels, what they need, how you can best deal with them. It may be the reason you can write great songs, be a fantastic coach or create beautiful poetry. Of course that doesn't suddenly make what happened to you good, but it does make it not *just* bad. It's all a matter of how you want to look at it. I believe that the toughest times also give us our greatest strengths. We should cherish the strength we learned from those experiences.

Maybe you currently feel like you're doing well and want to get to know yourself a little better. Understanding your past certainly helps with that. Maybe you feel like you're not quite on your path yet or don't even know where to start. Understanding your past is going to help you feel better, and better align your life with who you are. Whether you look back on your past with a sense of peace or still feel a lot of turmoil, what I want is for you to eventually get to a place where your past is no longer keeping you trapped in a version of yourself that you no longer are and that doesn't have your best interests at heart. Nor do I want the past to hold you captive in a life that no longer suits you. You deserve so much more! You know who stands in your way to stop you from staying true to yourself and living the life you want? You do. After all, it is much easier to break patterns when you get to know yourself better. So that's what we are going to do, step by step, with every page you read in this book.

TODAY

The desires and expectations we have today are shaped by our earliest experiences. What did your parents or caregivers do? What did they like? What didn't they like? What got their approval? What did they disapprove of? How did they speak to themselves? How did they speak to you? What intense experiences did you go through? All these things influence your choices for better and for worse. Often, we unconsciously, but also consciously, repeat our past. We keep doing what we learned when we were young, or maybe we react by doing the exact opposite. All these experiences influence our judgment more than we think. Seeing and understanding your past is the most important step to finding more peace and balance in the present and in a brighter future. And again, not by fiddling with it indefinitely. Coming back to the IKEA cabinet: why would you want to take it apart countless times? It will only cause lots of stress and hassle, it will remain the same cabinet and it will probably only look worse as more and more parts break and get lost each time you disassemble it. You only need to repair the drawer if you're constantly annoyed by the way it squeaks every time you pull it out. If a drawer is too full, throw some junk out so you have space for the things you actually need. What do you want with that cabinet right now and what needs to be fixed to get to that goal? What do you want to change in your life today, and what needs to be fixed for you to get there? Understanding how your past has shaped you helps you better understand why you are where you are today. So that's what we're going to focus on now. Who are you? How do you think? How do you feel? How do you behave? And what are you struggling with that you would like to change? Once again you're going to get to know yourself a little better.

Maybe you are currently happy with your life; you know yourself well and you know exactly what you want. Maybe you're not so happy with yourself and you don't know what to do about it. Maybe you have wanted to make a move for some time, but you keep hesitating. Should you finally switch jobs? Or take that leap in your love life. Or do something completely different than you would expect with your studies, or maybe you want a divorce? Whatever it is, wanting it is one thing. Doing it is another. Because then all kinds of fears and doubts suddenly appear out of nowhere. Can I do it? Will I manage? It's not supposed to be this way, is it? What will other people think? Or maybe you have persistent patterns that cause those good intentions to fail before you even get started, because dealing with situations in a certain way is so ingrained into your system. To better understand where you are today, I want to talk about two important things that are currently blocking you: labels and coping. In simple terms, who do you think you are and how do you deal with stress?

Let's start with labels. Maybe you struggle with feelings of low self-esteem. Usually this is not something that happened recently, but something that you have been carrying around with you for a lifetime. It can be the same with people pleasing. Why do you care so well for others but not for yourself? Is that something new or is it because the part of you that needed to be taken care of is trying to heal? For example, you may have regularly heard from others that you should just shut up or that you will never make it. That you are shy, lazy, or clumsy. That you are too busy, hypersensitive or introverted. Because others repeatedly tell you who you are, especially if they are people who are or were important to you, you get a little confused about what you think about yourself. It won't take long until you think "if they say so, it must be so." In fact, often we'll repeat it ourselves. "Oh, I'm really a disorganized person. I'm so ugly. I'm way too shy for that. No, I can't speak in front of large groups. I probably won't be able to do it, I'm not smart enough for that. Crying is weak; I have to be strong. I always let people walk all over me." If you tell yourself something often enough, you

You're not lost. You are
here. And if you can only see your
next step, that's enough.

automatically start to believe it. And you start to live by it. Not putting on that dress, because I can't wear things like that. Not asking for that salary increase, because who am I? Not expressing your feelings and asking for help, because you should be able to solve it yourself. Not pursuing your passion, because then you'd have to stand in front of a group, and you can't do something like that. Which of course is nonsense. There is nothing inherent in you that prevents you from doing these things. It's not that you have a gene that makes you "disorganized" or "shy", that that "is who you are" and that you have to just accept that. You don't. Because you know what that is? It's just a label. A label others put on you, or maybe you put on yourself, so that you fit into a box. A label that you have repeated so often that now you believe it and live by it. And the annoying thing is, often we are not even aware of it. Which is quite silly. If I tell you, "Tell yourself you're a tomato a hundred times," and then I ask "Are you a tomato?" You would laugh in my face, right? Of course, you're not a tomato! But if you tell yourself you're shy a hundred times, don't you start to believe it the 101st time? Would you say '"what are you talking about? I'm very social, I just like to surround myself with people I feel comfortable with." Or would you come to believe it? And perhaps start behaving accordingly? Probably yes. Many studies have demonstrated this fact. Tell two randomly selected groups that one is better at math than the other, then give them some equations to solve, and the people in the group who *think* they are better will perform better. Time after time, the randomly selected group performs better just because they have been told "they are better." We believe what we think and we feel and behave accordingly. So all those labels you use for yourself, all the boxes you put yourself into, they will continue to define you, until you say "stop, this is not who I am." Don't believe everything you think. Dare to question it. Especially if it only brings you down!

Now write them down, all your "I am's." Once you have your list, see which ones are positive, which ones you are proud of, the ones that help you move forward in life. You want to cherish those. But also decide which ones are negative, don't help you move forward and mainly keep you in your place, instead of allowing you to grow. We want to throw those on the trash heap. The way you think about yourself, is how you will be. If you give yourself labels, then you are going to live by them, because you keep repeating them. That becomes your reality. So, if you tell yourself "I can't stand up for myself," then you won't be able to stand up for yourself. If you tell yourself, you are a doubter, then you remain a doubter and you are never going to live decisively. You live by your labels. But you may be sticking those labels on yourself. It's almost never your genes. It's a choice. Maybe you don't know any other way because that's what you've been taught all your life, but that doesn't make it so. You are choosing these labels yourself, so you can choose who you want to be. "I'm a doubter." That's behavior that you chose. You could also choose a different label for yourself "I'm good at making choices." And then implement a plan for how you are going to get better at making choices. Naturally, you'll get better at doing so. Or maybe you tell yourself, "I'm a disorganized person." You choose to leave everything lying around because that fits perfectly with your label. You can also say "I'm organized," and implement a system like an organized person would. For example: I clean out all my old mail every week and I always put my keys in the same spot. It's a choice to let all your mail go unread or to randomly toss your keys somewhere and then forget where they are. If you enjoy all that stress, *be my guest*. But if that behavior doesn't make you a nicer person and it drives you crazy, or you want to be more orderly because you have future plans where being organized will come in handy, change it! You are not exactly like your father. You are not exactly like your mother. You are defined by your labels. You are what you tell yourself you are. *Know* yourself and stick to the labels that you feel really suit you. And if that's something negative like "I'm no master chef," that's totally fine. You don't have to excel at everything or want to work on everything. The bottom line is, you get to choose!

There is another thing that stops us from being who we want to be and dealing with situations in the ways that we would like. Those are our coping mechanisms. Your coping style is the way you tend to deal with setbacks and stressful circumstances. I often say: the problem is not the problem; the problem is how you *deal* with the problem. The way you deal with the problem is your coping mechanism. What you do when confronted with setbacks or stressful circumstances determines what effect the problem has on you. Most people have multiple coping styles – which is smart, because there are different situations, so the same one is not always effective – but you usually have one preference that best fits your character. I guess it's no surprise that your coping style is usually another souvenir you've brought back from your past. How did the authority figures in your life deal with challenges? How did you deal with those authority figures to feel as safe and loved as possible? What did you experience? We learn our coping strategies, healthy and unhealthy, from these experiences. Unhealthy coping strategies will often make you feel better in the moment, but often have long-term negative consequences. For example, drinking a glass of wine after a stressful day. You immediately feel more relaxed, but soon you need several glasses to really relax. The next morning you're annoyed because you didn't wake up feeling refreshed. Healthy coping strategies may not always feel good in the moment, but they do contribute to positive changes in the long run. It's not always pleasant to share with others that you're going through a hard time. It's scary to be vulnerable and ask for help, but afterwards you'll feel relief, and your vulnerability will strengthen those relationships with the people who supported you through those tough times. It also ensures that you can handle the next storm.

We all have stress and setbacks in life. Your way of dealing with them can make your life a lot harder or easier. Ask yourself: what exactly is your way of dealing with stress? How do you deal with confrontations or difficult situations? There are many ways of coping. I will list some of the most common ones to provide some examples. Numbing is one method: distracting yourself from the problem with alcohol and drugs, or losing yourself in work or sex. Actively address and solve: you think about what the options are in terms of a solution and make a choice based on that. Avoidance: pretending the problem doesn't exist and moving comfortably around it. Seeking social support: you seek help, comfort, understanding or support from others. Powerless passivity or depressive reaction pattern: lingering in brooding, doubting, and blaming yourself. Expressing your emotions: something you can of course do in healthy, but also in unhealthy ways. Do you engage in conversation or just scream curse words? The last coping method I will mention here is reassuring thoughts: you calm yourself by putting the situation in perspective and looking at it positively. Could it have been worse? What are the positives? What can you learn from this? There are plenty of other coping styles, but I'm not expecting you to write a perfect essay on the subject. I want you to think about how you handle difficult situations – situations that make you anxious, nervous, insecure, sad or angry – and whether you are currently acting the way you want to act or if there is room for growth, so that you can stay more true to yourself and live your life the way you want to live it.

The first thing you have to do if you want to improve your coping skills, is to recognize exactly what causes your stress and how you react to it. How do you cope now? Is it in a positive or negative way? Does it benefit you in the long run or not? Be honest with yourself. Yes, it can be nice to bury your head in the sand, yes, it can feel good to call someone names, and yes, it might be nice to pour yourself that glass of wine, but is that really what you want? Are you really helping yourself by doing that? Does it build your self-confidence? Is it the best way to process your emotions? Is that how you create deeper connections with others? If it's not working for you, try something else. We are all so afraid of experiencing temporary discomfort, when in fact that is the only way to feel comfortable in the long-term. This is also exactly what you learn in therapy, for example, when dealing with a panic attack. Instead of running away from the supermarket because you panic there and think you're going to have a heart attack, you stay. You tell yourself that you're not dying, and you stay until you notice that the anxiety subsides and you recognize that it's temporary. You do something different, often the exact opposite, of what you would normally do, and it works wonderfully. Does it feel good in the moment? No. Does it feel good in the long run? Yes! In these moments you really choose for yourself, what you *really* need to feel good. But this also works in other scenarios. Maybe your coping mechanism is withdrawal. Whenever you get into arguments in your relationship you shut down. Well then, the trick is to do things differently now. For once, don't walk away, but engage in a conversation. Try to make sense of what's going through your head. And of course, if you've always done things a certain way, that feels like the easiest way, even though you know it probably won't work in the long run. Challenge yourself to experience some short-term discomfort for once to make your life that much easier in the long run.

Again, one of the best things I've taught myself in life is to ask myself more often: why am I doing what I'm doing? So when you react a certain way to a situation, consciously ask yourself: why am I doing this? What do I want to achieve? Can I do it differently and choose myself and the things that I really need more? Your reaction wants to tell you something, listen to that. I often hear people say, "I have anxiety, I have panic attacks, I feel burned out or I have depression." Yes, that's the diagnosis a professional has made or the label you've put on yourself. But they are the result of something else. What's behind them? Maybe that fear, that stress and fatigue, or that panic is your way of dealing with a loss? A trauma? An anxious thought in your head? Or pressure to perform? Why do you get that panic attack? Why do you feel so gloomy? Why are you completely spent and exhausted? It's your current way of dealing with a stressful situation. What is that situation? Resolve it; how you think about it, how you feel about it, how you act. When we deal with that stressful situation, that reaction that you feel as a consequence, goes away.

Most physical and psychological complaints that people experience originate in losing sight of who you are and what you want. What do you really want? When you're burned out you don't really want to rest, you just don't want to carry the cares of the whole world on your shoulders any longer. You no longer want to feel guilty when you take a rest. You want to chart your own course in your career. You want to listen to your heart more. These days we almost think that we *are* our diagnoses, our labels. By now you understand we are not. What are our symptoms, our reactions, our feelings, and our bodies trying to do? They are trying to tell us something. And it's time to start listening to what exactly they are trying to tell us! And to choose better ways to deal with them.

Now that we have talked about labels and coping, it is important to zoom in on who you really are. To get to know your real self a little better, it is important to answer some questions. As much as possible, try to let go of what others think, or expect and just answer from the heart. Answer with whatever comes to mind first, because usually that is not yet colored by other voices. Describe yourself in five words. Ask yourself if your personality has changed since childhood. What have you adopted from your father or mother, for example? On the other hand, what do you do completely differently? What qualities do you value most in yourself right now? What are your strengths? What are your weaknesses? Which qualities do you value in others, and which do you not? Which qualities do you value in yourself and which qualities do you not feel so good about? What are you interested in? And now think about

Only you know how hard you have worked to get where you are today. Think of all the challenges you've overcome and all the times when you thought you couldn't do something. And yet, here you are. You can be proud of yourself. I hope you give yourself the credit you deserve.

your life. What do you not want that you do have now? What do you want that you don't have now? As you open your calendar for the next seven days, ask yourself, what energizes you and what are you looking forward to? And what drains you? How do you spend your free time? What dreams and goals do you have? And why are these important to you? What is currently stopping you from going for what you want? What are the most important things in your life right now? And then when you look at how you spend your time each week, are you aligned with what is most important to you, or should you start prioritizing different things?

If you find it difficult to answer these questions about yourself and your life, let those around you help. The point is not to let others define who you are, the point is that if you ask their opinion and are open to feedback, you can find out things that you may not have realized about yourself. And that's also why you shouldn't just ask anyone, but only the people who you feel have your best interests at heart. For example, ask your best friend, your sibling, mother, or father how they see your character. You don't have to agree with everything they say, it just has to get you thinking. Is there a grain of truth in it? Can I do something with this? Do I want to do something with this? Well, that's enough questions about who you are as a person.

The next thing I want to ask you is: if there were anything you could change about yourself or your life today, what would it be? Think about that for a moment. Write it down. What comes to mind first? Make a list of all the things you would like to change in your life, and now pinpoint the problem: What is holding you back? Is it those labels? Is it your way of coping? What exactly are the obstacles? What is the deeper cause behind them? And now look at those obstacles again. What is really causing them? Are you in an unhealthy relationship because you're unlucky or because you've deluded yourself into thinking you can't get anything better? Are you not getting opportunities at work or are you just afraid to ask and fail? Do people shut you out or do you just find it hard to make deeper connections and maybe that requires growth on your end? You are the product of everything you have experienced in your life. You have learned from your parents' experiences and now it is time to learn from your own. Learn what is causing your pain so you can create your new future.

YOUR FUTURE

One of the easiest things you can do is to stay exactly where you are. If you are who you want to be and you are living the life you want, I would definitely recommend you keep doing that. But what if you have dreams? What if you feel trapped in the space between who you are and who you want to be? What if you want to do things differently? Maybe you only want a small change. Maybe you have bigger desires. The fact is that more people choose the uncomfortable known than the comfortable unknown. Well, this job may not be what makes me happy, but I make a living. Well, this relationship isn't what I want, but what if I wind up alone forever? We choose comfort and safety over happiness. Because it's nice to be in a situation that is familiar and comforting. At least then you know exactly where you stand. But also know the price that you pay: your happiness.

What if you do go out of that comfort zone? What if your inner voice repeatedly whispers: "this job won't make you happy" or "this friendship isn't good for you" or "you're worthy of being truly loved" or "go make that business idea a reality." What if that voice has been whispering for so long that by now it's screaming. DO SOMETHING! ANYTHING! This is not you! This is not what you want! Do you dare go out of your comfort zone? There is a question that can really help you if you find it scary to venture into new territory. Ask yourself: what is the very worst thing that could happen? Try to visualize your worst-case scenario and then ask yourself: okay, and if that happens, then what? What happens next? I'll bet that nine times out of ten it isn't that bad at all. No, change doesn't always feel good, but do you know what *really* doesn't feel good? Being stuck somewhere you don't belong anymore. That's just the worst! Not daring to switch careers because it might not work out? There are plenty of jobs out there. If you are not lazy, you can make a living. You might have to hop between jobs a few times to get where you want to be, but *who cares*? You know by now that you're going to learn a lot from the experience and you can come out on the other side even better, right? Not daring to say goodbye to a bad relationship because you are afraid you'll end up alone? There are seven billion people in the world. Seven!!! Time to give yourself a little more credit. If you're not happy, break up! Instead of thinking about all the ways that things can go wrong and exaggerating the possible negative consequences in your mind, try thinking more in terms of opportunities and possibilities rather than problems and obstacles. Whether you believe you can or can't do something, you'll be right either way. I would go for the option that gives you the chance for a brighter future. My personal rule of thumb is that as long as I'm not likely to die doing this thing, I might as well try it. So, instead of asking yourself what could go wrong, ask what could go right. Ask yourself: what could happen that could greatly benefit me? What do I have to gain? Imagine choosing a fulfilling career path that gives you everything you want from your work. How would that change your life? How would the people you care about benefit from this? If you do something with enthusiasm, whatever it is, not only will it give you more satisfaction and happiness, but you're also much more likely to succeed. What would happen if you moved to that place you always wanted to live? What if you pursue your love life in a way that makes you happy instead of how other people think it should be? What if you start taking more time for yourself and saying, "fuck it, I'll just do it!" more often. You'll always miss the shots you don't take. Once you start thinking this way you'll be amazed at your own potential. And how much you can achieve in a short time.

People often tell me, "I've been thinking about this for so long, I just don't know what to do." Well, if you keep thinking about it, it's not so hard, you already have your answer! In any case, your doubt means that you realize that where you are now is no longer

There is no *one size fits all.*
Focus on your happiness, whatever
that looks like to you.

what you want. Suppose you have doubts about whether you should continue with your relationship. I'm the first to say that it's not a good idea to make big changes overnight. But if this doubt comes back repeatedly in your life, you have to ask yourself if this is the right place for you. The truth is you already know that it is not. Your doubt is mainly fear of what is to come, but you know deep inside yourself that where you are now no longer works for you.

A fun way to think about your future without the limitations of patterns, fears, doubts, or obstacles is to do the miracle thought exercise. When we are looking for a solution to a problem, we tend to focus on the problem in front of us. Why something will or won't work. Instead, what you want to do is ignore all the problems that might get in the way of your goal and look purely at the result. You want to formulate exactly what it is you want to achieve. How exactly you are going to achieve that is a problem for later. The exercise is as follows: imagine that you are leading your normal life and going to sleep as usual. You are not aware that something happens at night: a miracle. Exactly what you hoped would change about yourself or your life has happened. But the funny thing is, when you wake up the next day, you don't know that a miracle has happened. After all, you were asleep. The fact is: the problem you were facing no longer exists. Suppose you start your day now: what would be the very first difference you would notice in your life? How do you know the miracle has happened? What differences do you notice in your thoughts? How do you feel? What emotions do you experience? What are you doing? What is your behavior? What type of person are you? How do your friends, parents, partner, or children know something has happened? What do they notice about you? What would you do next with your day? If we were to compare your life before and after the miracle, what is the difference? What has changed in you as a person and in your life? Many of us focus only on problems that get in the way of our happiness and not on what our life would look like once we find the solutions. The miracle question helps you uncover your limiting beliefs. To start living as if the miracle happened. To start thinking, feeling, and behaving that way. A lot of people say: first I need to see it and then I will believe it. No, in fact, for many changes in our lives it is important to first start believing and living as if it has already happened, then you will start seeing it naturally. Use the miracle question and everything it teaches you to be the person you want to be, until you are that person. Learn to think in terms of possibilities instead of obstacles. When you start thinking this way, it becomes much easier to find possible routes to that final destination.

When you look at your future it's not about seeing what you like about yourself and what you don't, what you're good at and what you suck at, and that you have to turn all those minuses into pluses. You don't have to excel in everything, you don't have to like everything about yourself. It's all about awareness. Then change what stands in the way of you being who you want to be. If you like being by yourself and you're not a social creature, that's totally okay. Or you may want to develop that side of yourself more because you crave more connection. If you hate cooking, that's okay. It's not a bad thing to have someone else do it, order take away more often or stick to simple dishes. Or maybe you enjoy developing that skill. Then focus on it. To know yourself is to *see* yourself. Your positives as well as your negatives. And working on the things you want to work on, because it lets you be the person you want to be. Put your energy into where your strengths lie and what makes you happy. Actively determine who you are and where you want to go with your life.

Knowing yourself and finding your own path can be quite a tricky one because it is very easy to get lost in the views and opinions of those around you. It's important to start walking your own path at some point. When you don't know yourself, you run the risk of becoming alienated from yourself. A gap is

The only certainty we have in life is that it will all be over one day. And when that day comes you won't give a flying fuck about how hard you've worked, what your mom's friend thought about your love life, how many likes you got on that post or if your butt looked good in low rise jeans. It will all be over one day and the only thing that will matter to you is if you lived a life that is true to yourself and if you spent enough time with your loved ones. Build your life accordingly.

then created between you and your daily life. Then you start finding yourself in situations that make you feel sad, guilty, ashamed, or overwhelmed. You get stuck in work that you don't enjoy, friendships that don't bring you anything or maybe even undermine you. Are you not getting what you need out of life? Or perhaps you feel like you must get everything out of it, while your true self needs more rest and relaxation. This is exactly why we have already made considerable strides in self-discovery. You know where you came from and where you are today. When we talk about your future, I want us to look at who you want to be and where you want to be. And even though such a chapter on "me, me, me" may feel selfish, it certainly isn't. The impact that knowing yourself has on others is huge. In a positive sense. The more authentic you are, the more valuable you can be as a parent, friend, colleague, partner, family or community member.

You now have an idea of where you came from, where you are now and where you are going. And you can come back to this over and over again when you are dealing with big events or when a certain phase in life calls for it. You can do this when you feel good and want to hold on to that feeling. Or in those moments when you think you've lost yourself or lost your way a bit. Getting to know yourself is a lifelong process, not something you complete in an hour. Every day you should intentionally be curious about yourself. To feel: I want to rediscover myself every day, for a lifetime. Not by therapizing for hours every day, but simply by living consciously every day. What do I think about this? What do I want from this? Why am I doing this? To ask yourself those questions more often, possibly every day, when you think, feel, and do things. It helps you to get to know yourself more and more. And the great thing is, once you know who you are, you don't want to be anyone but that person.

BEING YOURSELF

You are not who you are.
You are not who others say you are.
You are who you choose to be.

FEELING, DEALING, HEALING

Knowing yourself is knowing your past, where you are today and where you want to go in the future. Being yourself means leaving behind what no longer serves you and focusing on where you *do* want to go. Feeling, dealing and healing is a very important part of this, because as long as you remain triggered by and continue to act upon old patterns, labels and traumas, you do not allow yourself to be who you want to be now. You will keep repeating old behaviors that no longer help you move forward, and you will keep seeing yourself through old filters that no longer work for you. And you may not always do this consciously, but subconsciously. That's the tricky thing with beliefs or set ways of doing things: they become automatic. Awareness is an important step in breaking those kinds of automatic responses, something we worked on in the previous chapter. The challenge is to process the accompanying emotions, so that you create peace of mind for yourself and a fresh start to being yourself.

Many people find it difficult to really feel and express their emotions. Because we never learned how to do it, because we don't feel safe enough, because it used to be something we were punished for, or because we're afraid of what might happen if we start doing this now and *really* have to face up to everything that's happened. Emotions are healthy and human, and in some situations they're extremely useful. They help us communicate with other people and ourselves, they help us to react appropriately to different situations, they enable us to really experience things, and, more importantly, emotions help us survive. But emotions can also frustrate us if we hide them or don't understand them. Then they keep popping up at moments we don't want them to, because they don't really fit the situation at all. And that's why you often hear people make annoying comments like "come on, get over it". Easier said than done. Ever tried shoving a trauma into the back of a kitchen cabinet? It will break all your fancy china in no time. So, let me explain how you can make sure the past doesn't keep blocking you from being yourself today. Some people call it healing, others call it shadow work or trauma processing. For me, it's a combination of doing things that just work, so that you can stay true to yourself and start living life the way you want to.

When you want to change something, first you have to understand where it came from. That's how it works with emotions, too. The next step is learning to deal with them in a helpful way. Finally, we want to give our emotions space so that we do not suffer from them again and again. So, feeling, dealing, and healing involves three steps. First, acknowledge and recognize the emotion. Next, deal with it adequately. Finally, make sure that the emotion is resolved, so that it bothers you as little as possible in your daily life. This process also touches on your coping behavior, which we talked about earlier. Do you remember your way of reacting to stressful situations? Like maybe hiding your feelings or pretending they don't exist? Or maybe reacting very intensely? Do you recognize this way of thinking, feeling or acting from the past? Does something in the situation you're facing today trigger old pain? Or is it an emotion that actually just fits this moment and that you *are allowed to* feel? Of course, you're always allowed to feel anything you want, but I'm assuming you don't always like having a very intense reaction to things that may not actually be that intense at all. Maybe you are overly concerned about what your neighbor thinks of you. Or setbacks feel devastating. Maybe you are never truly able to enjoy those moments when you think you should be feeling happy, because you keep worrying about everything and nothing. Often this is because situations consciously or unconsciously remind us of situations from the past and evoke the same emotions. Emotions that aren't really called for anymore, but that you have taken with you as a souvenir from a period that is now behind you.

It's a lot easier to
find yourself if you've lost
yourself first.

Suppose you were a sensitive child. When something happened, you reacted emotionally and were often told: "Stop crying already, you're acting up, everything is fine!" That's when you started suppressing your sensitive side and why you wanted to be "tough" above all else. After all, in your childhood you received praise when you were a tough cookie. So you learned to ignore your emotions more and more. In adulthood, you are confronted with the consequences: a partner who doesn't get you, for example, because you're not showing your emotions. Or you find it difficult to truly enjoy and experience positive emotions, and therefore never really feel happy. And when something awful happens – for example, the death of a friend – you might discover you can't even cry. The moment something does really get to you, you immediately clam up and hide your tears away. Because it still feels as if those emotions aren't allowed to be there. When you allow yourself to observe this, you start connecting the dots. "Hey, I've taught myself that emotions are bad and that's why I now find it difficult to access my emotions when something happens. But I do actually want to be able to feel more, to enjoy the wonderful moments and to deal with things that suck. I understand that blocking my emotions is my coping mechanism, but I no longer want that. And I also no longer want to live by the condition of worth that "If I want to be of value, I have to be tough." I just want to be able to be myself."

Really feeling our emotions can be very tough when we see them as negative. Why not grant your body and mind the relief of finding closure? Ask yourself why you struggle to acknowledge certain emotions, or emotions in general? What is the root cause? What are you afraid of? What is the worst thing that can happen if you allow yourself to feel that way? Again, you will have to ask yourself: "Why exactly am I doing what I'm doing?" And then it's very important to consider what you need to do in order to heal. Our emotions send us signals that something is right or wrong. You're only hurting yourself when you don't listen to your emotions. You're not enjoying the good things and you aren't dealing with the negative stuff either. And no, suppressing your emotions doesn't make you stronger. On the contrary, ignoring your emotions makes you extremely vulnerable. It means you can be triggered by anything and everything; it makes you very unstable. Strong people are actually the ones who are in touch with their emotions. Being sensitive and daring to be vulnerable – now that's a superpower. If you don't acknowledge the emotions associated with everything that has happened in your life, you are in fact not acknowledging a part of yourself. If you want to be yourself, you must stop hiding in every possible way. Whether it's anxiety, stress, or depression, there's a reason you feel that way. If you dare to look at *the good, the bad and the ugly* and seek healing, you will see that these feelings no longer prevent you from being who you want to be, allowing you to shape your future. If you don't process pain, you will keep on being scared of certain situations. And that sensitivity prevents you from growing. You start making choices based on fear, and that's not what you want. You want to start trusting yourself. If you don't process anger, you will continue to feel angry.

Don't forget that the most important thing for healing is awareness. Acknowledge and accept the existence of something. If a child asks you a question, but you don't respond, what do they usually do? They repeat the question. And again. And again. And again. And at some point, they start yelling to get your attention, grabbing your arm, and kicking your leg. "You're not listening!" Unprocessed emotions work the same way. It starts with a whisper, but if you don't listen, soon you'll find yourself breaking into tears when someone gives you constructive feedback because you never healed from the fact that your parents were so critical of you as a child. Your emotional reaction – that can be tears, but also anger and everything in between – to your colleague saying, "next time it would be nice if you would just put that report in the right spot," is disproportionate to what is really happening. You still have feelings about this subject that you need to process if you don't want to immediately turn back into that child at such moments. You want to have moments of growth and be able to receive feedback confidently, without immediately doubting yourself. So that's why you want to work on healing, so that you can let old wounds rest and so that it doesn't feel as if someone is poking at them every time you have to deal with anything that touches on those old traumas, and those unhealed injuries become open wounds again. When you let a wound heal, the scar remains, but it is no longer bleeding, infected and painful. Not even if someone touches it once in a while.

Now write down what emotions you feel about the past. That can be anything, from your childhood to where you are right now. Acknowledge those emotions. Write down what you understand about yourself that triggers this emotion and why it is so important to let it go. The basic sentence structure you can use is ''I understand that I am feeling X because… I am going to heal this part of me because… After all, I now know that…" For example: *I understand that I feel attacked and inferior because the fact that my colleague is criticizing me brings me back to those moments as a child and all the emotions I felt back then. It reminds me of the way my parents told me I hadn't done something right.*

That I couldn't do something. That I would never succeed. I am going to heal this part of me because I no longer want to be held captive by old pain. I want to be able to receive feedback because that is an opportunity for me to learn and grow. Criticism says nothing about me as a person. I now know that I am worth it. I am smart, strong and I have it in me to achieve whatever I want to achieve. I don't need to be more than I am now. I am always worth it.

Feeling, dealing and healing is the moment where you once again hold your backpack upside down and throw some crap out. And that can be anything. You can write down all kinds of feelings here, from shame to guilt to anger, disappointment, pain, fear or insecurity. The important thing is not to judge, but to simply observe these feelings. It is about acknowledging your emotions and understanding why they are there, but also understanding why it is so important for you to deal with them and let them go. By really feeling and acknowledging your emotions and giving your feelings room to breathe, you are healing. Very often we want to hide these emotions away or deny them, or we get bogged down in blame and pointing fingers at others, which prevents us from letting go. That doesn't help us move forward. By doing so, we don't solve anything. After all, pointing fingers does not mean that we will also get the apology we want.

Perhaps the other person is not capable of that at all or is not even alive anymore. It's a harsh reality, but remember that whatever was done to you, by anyone, even if you yourself are not at all to blame for what happened, you still have the responsibility to resolve it. It affects you. So don't let someone else hold the key to solving your problems. You won't be the first person to spend a lifetime waiting for an apology, for someone else to reach out to you or offer a solution, which will never come, or only in a way that doesn't help you at all. Putting your healing journey on pause or completely ignoring the healing process does not make it go away. It's like a toddler who holds their hands in front of their eyes and says: "'I don't see you, so you don't see me either. I'm not here." Unfortunately, that's not how it works in real life. Your feelings exist and the emotions you are experiencing want to tell you something. It is the child in you begging for your attention. And it shows up at the craziest times. Listen. Acknowledge. And observe without judgment. That's all you have to do. Feeling, dealing, and healing is the way to take back control over yourself. You have to be the key to the solution yourself. And completing this exercise will help you because once you acknowledge what that child in you wants to tell you, it feels heard and seen. YOU feel heard and seen. And then there is no need for yelling or kicking you in the shins. At some point even whispers won't be necessary anymore.

At some point, that child in you thinks "actually, I've had my say. I'm good". So, you can just *be*. As I said before, no one comes out of the struggle of this life unscathed. We all go through things. Realize that trauma creates change that you didn't choose. Healing, on the other hand, creates change that you do choose.

When you're able to get rid of all the old shit, you can work toward something new. As far as I'm concerned, feeling, dealing and healing is also about acknowledging your own share in the things that have happened in your life. It's not just about healing from what others have done to you, but also healing from those moments when you made things difficult for yourself or others. It also means reflecting on your actions and being able to say "I didn't do this right," or "I hurt someone by doing that." It can be a huge relief when you're able to apologize to yourself or others. Owning up to mistakes and forgiving yourself allows you to move on. You are not your mistakes. Acknowledge them. And forgive yourself. Take the lesson with you. Do you still need to make strides to get where you want to be? Are there people who immediately come to mind that you need to talk to? Then go talk to them. Get over your shame and guilt. Even if that person is no longer around or not open to it: write a letter and speak your mind. Whether you let someone else read it, or you burn it to leave it

Just do it.
And if you're scared? Then
just do it scared!

behind you, you have to move on. It's going to help you. You're never going to be able to be yourself if you can't let go of what's behind you. That's why this tough part is so important when you decide to really start choosing yourself.

Empty the cup! This is a beautiful quote about healing from the famous monk, Shi Heng Yi. His idea: the only way to let something that is blocked flow again, is to say goodbye to old things so that something new can come into your life. Simply put, sometimes you must pour the old tea in your cup down the drain and fill it with fresh new tea. And then suddenly look very different. Often, we tend to hold on to what we know, but the fact that something is familiar, and therefore predictable, certainly doesn't necessarily mean that what we know is always good for us. Starting over is scary, but those who dare to do it are often richly rewarded by life. *Just empty the cup.*

If you incorporate all the tools we've discussed in this book and then think, "Hm, I must be doing something wrong, I feel so crappy, I feel different, I feel distant from people, I want to be on my own," then give yourself applause. That's a sign you are doing *exactly* what is needed. We always talk about healing as if it's a wonderful process, but it isn't. The result is beautiful, sure, but on your healing journey you will often look like shit. It's not like the *healing journeys* you see on social media: start your day at 6 a.m. with some journaling, yoga and a cold bath, and you'll feel reborn. Chances are you'd rather stay in bed because you no longer enjoy the things you thought you enjoyed. Or you feel like an outsider or lonely because you're outgrowing people. Healing is acknowledging your own bullshit excuses, being ashamed of the things you've done because you didn't know any better, and making progress, only to fall flat on your face again. Does that feel good? No. Are you on the right track? Yes. A good indicator that you're really on your healing journey, is not feeling good precisely because you're becoming the person you've always wanted to be. And that involves things like standing up for yourself, having difficult conversations and saying goodbye to people. It's not all fun and games. Healing is hard work and some of your old injuries may flare-up again, but being healed is a beautiful thing. You'll naturally come to experience that. Because you'll feel more self-confident and so much more balanced. You will notice that your relationship with yourself and others is so much deeper and more loving. You will notice how much more creative you are and how strong you feel, both mentally and physically. You will feel much more confident when making choices, trusting yourself that you are making the right choice – because you're listening more closely to your own inner voice instead of the voices in the world around you. You will feel so much calmer and more peaceful in just about everything you do. Once you know, are and choose yourself there is *no way back*, because it is the best feeling imaginable.

In the end, we all tell ourselves stories about who we are and who we are not and why we can or cannot accomplish things. As long as you remain stuck in an old story about yourself and do not really feel it, deal with it and heal it, you cannot create a new story. Then you will remain stuck in your past: in your divorce, in the grief of loss, in feeling excluded, feeling worthless, feeling codependent, needy, or becoming defensive. And that means you will stay stuck in the old version of yourself and a future that belongs to that version of you. Feeling, dealing and healing helps you to stay away from unhelpful thoughts, feelings and reactions. It helps you to get new core beliefs and effective ways of responding to situations that align with your happiness. Realize that if you don't pay proper attention to old pains, they will continue to have a negative impact by working their way into your life over and over again. Once you focus on healing and what the past has taught you, you grow. Until your old story no longer has a hold of you. That is the moment when you will hear yourself say, "That was the old me, but that is not who I am anymore. I'm staying true to myself now."

EMBRACING CHANGE

Whether you like it or not, your life is going to change, both in ways you welcome and in ways you would never choose. From very small changes, such as canceling an appointment, to major life-changing events, such as losing something or someone. You have probably had to deal with all these sorts of changes at some point in your life. The question is: Do you know how to surrender to those changes? Can you embrace change, or do you resist? The fact is you can't avoid it. You can't say "no, not this change, no thank you.. I'll take the next one." Change is part of life. And most of the time there is no choice as to whether it happens. The only choice you have is how you deal with it. How you deal with change largely creates the impact it has on your life. Let me be clear; sometimes people have to endure terrible things for no good reason. It's completely understandable that some events have a major impact on your life. However, the hard part of life is that you just have to swallow the bitter pill. You have no choice but to deal with it because it *is* there. And so that's where the challenge lies: how do you deal with something bad in the best way possible? When you surrender to it, you will see that there are many opportunities in expected and unexpected, wanted, and unwanted changes. Every change brings lessons, wisdom and experience. And that is why people manage to find their greatest strength in their greatest misery. You can look at the problem, but you can also decide to look at the opportunity for growth. As you learn to deal better with change and the more often you initiate change yourself, the happier and more successful you will be. Because, only by embracing change can you really stay true to yourself.

Embracing change is easier said than done, especially when what is happening sucks with a capital S. But it does allow you to navigate unpleasant challenges that come your way in the best way possible. When you are faced with a challenge, observe what your reaction is. Often, it is in our nature to turn it into something negative, which has many disadvantages. Suppose your challenge is that the company you work for is going through a reorganization. Your first thought might be: I'm probably going to be one of the people getting fired. Or a different kind of challenge: I have decided to pursue my dream of living abroad. Your reaction could be: What if I risk my friendships by doing this? Instead of these reactions, you could also think, so what if I *do* get fired, it might be just the push I needed to finally start my own business, which I've been thinking about doing for ages. And if I end up living in a sunny

Getting what you want is about
having the courage to walk away. If you
want to welcome new things into your life,
you will have to let go of old things.

southern European country, my friends can visit me in the winter and we'll have more quality time in the winter sun. An important part of embracing change is looking at it with a positive mindset. Instead of thinking "I can't do it because others are better at it," think "I may need time to learn a thing or two, but I can do it. I'll give myself time to make it my own and ask for help when I need it." Instead of saying "I failed because I didn't get that job," you can think "I didn't succeed now, but I learned what I can do better next time. I'm sure this experience will help me succeed in the future." Instead of thinking "shit, she thinks I'm dull," you can also think, "*so what*, I happen to think I'm fantastic myself. Too bad she has such bad taste."' Problem solved. Lesson learned. Challenge embraced.

When we remain open to new opportunities and lessons, we allow ourselves to get to know new parts of ourselves and our lives. This makes you more flexible, and therefore more relaxed when faced with challenges. It will increase your self-confidence, composure, and strength. You'll learn to think and do new things, and develop new skills. It will help you reflect more often on who you really are and what you really think. It will give you a chance to develop your ideas and opinions and not become stuck in your ways. If there's anything you don't want, it's to become that aunt who makes the same speech again and again while everyone thinks "have you been living under a rock this whole time?" Or that uncle who is still hung up on how unfair it is that he got fired thirty years ago. *Life goes on!* Embracing change challenges you to look at something from a different perspective. The strongest people are those who accept that they don't really know anything for sure and are open to everything. The good and the bad. The great thing about change is that it will show you that you are much stronger and more resilient than you think. And that you can handle and achieve and do SO much more than you ever thought was possible. When you go through changes, and come out even stronger on the other side, it gives you the guts to take on new challenges and to be courageous in difficult times. It confirms that you're getting better at rolling with the punches, even when something completely unexpected happens. You'll never grow if you keep on doing the same thing. It is only when you challenge yourself that you learn great lessons. About yourself, others, and life. Often the strongest people are also the ones who have faced the most shit in their lives. If you have never experienced any adversity, a light breeze will knock you over. If you have been through a lot, you know how to navigate your way through the biggest storm, because your roots are deeply anchored in the soil. It makes you realize that you can survive anything life throws at you. You will also begin to appreciate the beauty in life more when you know it could be much worse. Obstacles only make the success that follows even more fulfilling, because you know what you had to do, leave behind and overcome to find that success. Feel free to look back and be proud of where you are today!

If you're thinking, "I don't know, I'm in so deep, I've really lost it", don't worry. Even though at such moments it might feel like things will never be right again, the opposite is true. Often the greatest breakthroughs in our lives are preceded by a massive breakdown. It is important to recognize that now, when you are feeling worse than ever, everything is shaky and uncertain and you may even feel like you are about to lose your mind, this is the moment that things are going to get better. This is the moment to say to yourself, "I know this will lead to a great breakthrough. When everything around me is a big mess, the eye of the storm can't be far away." Often the moment we question everything is also the moment we dare to rebuild our lives. It's only then that you can truly make a fresh start and create room for change. These moments force you to redefine everything. Think of it like you're redecorating a house. Sure, it looks nice when you just paint a wall, but what if you did a complete renovation. Pull everything out, put in a new foundation, rebuild all the walls? When you see a house that is being completely renovated and you are standing in the middle of that ruin, of course you think; "how is this ever going to be anything?" But when you see what you've accomplished after a year or so, with all the time, effort and love put into it, you think "wow, this is what I did it all for. This was so worth it. If only I could have seen then how beautiful it was going to be." The same thing is true when we're rebuilding ourselves. The moment when life is one big mess – whether that is literal or mainly in your head – when you are stressed, anxious or starting to panic, that is when you can reassess everything. Only then can you take the time to seriously answer the question, "Who am I and what do I really want?" And to say, "that window, I actually want that somewhere else" or "that person no longer fits into my life, because they simply don't have my best interests at heart." In retrospect people will often say "My lowest point turned out to be the beginning of a new life. It was painful, sad, fearful, and so much more, but I learned so much. It was truly a breakthrough. I now know exactly who I am and what I want out of my life." Sometimes life pushes you into uncomfortable positions, because otherwise you wouldn't have had the guts to move on.

When talking about embracing change, I cannot ignore the topic of grief. Too often grief is mis-interpreted. As if mourning is something you only experience when a loved one has died, when you literally lose someone. But mourning is actually a way to process the end of something important to you. This can apply to any loss in your life, not just the loss of a person who was important to you. So, any major change can cause mourning. It is a natural, emotional reaction that you can recognize by the feelings it stirs up; depression, numbness, anger, shame, guilt, confusion, jealousy and many other emotions. Maybe you feel everything very intensely or you feel nothing at all. Maybe you lock yourself in the house or you go the other way and just want to get out of the house. Maybe it gives you an unhealthy relationship with food: you eat way too much or can't get a bite down. Unprocessed grief makes you sleep poorly, affects your health and negatively impacts the way you make choices. That's why I want you to remember your grief. It is a normal response when you are going through changes, whatever they may be.

Imagine you have always wanted children and it turns out that it is not possible for you to have a child. This is a terrible and unexpected loss. It may feel like you've lost your vision of the future, your role as a parent, the baby you planned for, the family you could have had. This causes feelings of grief. When you have a child with a disability you might experience similar feelings. Not because you love your child any less, but because the life you saw before you suddenly looks different and you need time to process your new reality. So many other things can trigger feelings of mourning; becoming an empty nester when your children leave home, the illness of a partner, the loss of a relationship, the breakdown of a career or the end of a marriage or friendship. Or maybe the end of you, as the person you have always known yourself to be, because you face physical or mental challenges. Death is not the only form of loss. Loss of identity, security or income can trigger the same reaction. And it is not always related to negative events either. For example, motherhood and the loss of your old identity can also trigger a grief reaction. You can be happy with your new role and still mourn the fact that you are leaving a piece of yourself behind forever. Moving abroad is a positive event, but that doesn't mean you can't mourn the loss of your life as you knew it. All these changes and transitions can elicit a grieving process. If we understand grief and learn what kinds of life events can trigger these feelings, it becomes easier to deal with them. Too many people do not embrace these kinds of changes sufficiently, but it is necessary to prevent a physical or mental block. Grieving is about coping with loss and change. If you don't allow yourself to grieve about something, you deny yourself the ability to process that event. And you guessed it, it will keep coming back into your life until you do deal with it and it heals. Until you adapt to change, whether you wanted it or not.

Sometimes you are forced to change, sometimes you choose it. If there is one thing to remember, it is that you get to rewrite your story. Maybe you had all kinds of ideas about work, love, friendships, parenthood, where you wanted to live, or other parts of your life that no longer fit you. If so, you get to change that. In fact, not only is it okay to rearrange your life, sometimes it is necessary. Of course, sometimes you have to do things that you don't feel like doing, things that make you angry or sad, because that's just part of life and the only thing you can do then is roll up your sleeves and get it over with. But there are also times when you have to say, "hello, I'm not going to give up on being happy. This is not who I am anymore. This is not what I want anymore." If you can't let go of your past, you can't grow either. Don't live your life according to how you imagined or thought it should be if that doesn't make you happy anymore. Don't live your life according to other people's opinions or expectations either. It's okay to change, and change means venturing in unknown territory. You wouldn't tell a butterfly to stay a caterpillar just because that's what it was used to. Throw off that cocoon, spread your wings. If you want things to change, you have to have the courage to change yourself. Ask yourself: Are you really changing? Or are you just becoming more like the person you truly are?

There's a wonderful quote from Socrates. "The secret of change is not to put all your focus on fighting the old, but on building the new." Being yourself doesn't mean constantly thinking about what you don't want anymore, but mostly about thinking; what do I want? Who would I be if I were exactly who I wanted to be? How should I think if I am exactly who I want to be? What do I feel if I am exactly who I want to be? What actions do I take if I am exactly who I want to be? How do I deal with this challenge? We are so often stuck in what can't be that we forget to ask ourselves what can. And more importantly, we forget to live that way. It is important to understand that our brain is not designed to make us happy, it's designed for our survival. And that's why our minds get stressed or anxious very quickly if we don't learn to tame those little voices of worry. Fear keeps us safe; it's a warning signal from our survival instinct, but we have to judge whether the fear we feel is reasonable. What could really happen? Do you feel fear because the situation is actually life-threatening or is it about fear of what someone thinks of you, which may really feel frightening, but is not literally a matter of life or death. When is fear a good counselor (when a situation is life-threatening) and when is it not (in almost all other cases). Instead of automatically listening to your fears and allowing them to control your decisions, ask yourself: is this a well-founded fear or is this just nonsense? When does fear help you and when does it keep you stuck in the same place? This is a very important difference. The next time you feel fear of change, know that this is a natural and helpful emotion, but it doesn't always fit the situation. What can really happen? Worrying about "what will happen" and feeling excited about "what will happen" is a matter of mindset. It is a choice you can make. Get used to embracing change. Instead of seeing all the negatives, teach yourself to see the positives. Change what you feel so that instead of stress and anxiety you feel calmness, composure, and confidence that all will be well in the end. That YOU have it within you to make sure everything works out.

Something magical happens when you think "I'm going to choose myself." The end result, the happiness and meaning you get to experience in your life, is wonderful. The journey to get there? Not so much. It means saying goodbye to relationships, friends, situations, and circumstances. It begins the moment you are honest with yourself and start asking yourself "does this make me happy?" You can make that choice. And that doesn't mean that there's an ideal option right away, like moving on to your dream job or a perfect relationship. Sometimes It also means that you will have to go through a period where things get worse and your life feels unpleasant, to eventually get to where you want to be.

When you ask yourself "what do I really want?" that question can be overwhelming. But you can also ask yourself, "what can I do today to stay true to myself?" Take it step by step. It's a lot easier to make a small change that takes you in the direction you want to go. And the great part is this: if you keep making choices that are in line with your values, day after day, in all those small moments, one day you'll look up and realize that you've created the life you want. Imagine what would happen if every day you thought, "How can I help myself today, what do I need?" and you gave yourself that. Maybe you'll get some rest today instead of going to that party. Maybe you'll cook a healthy meal for yourself, instead of picking up greasy takeout. Maybe you'll start your day by journaling, instead of scrolling mindlessly on your phone for half an hour. Maybe in the evening you'll put your phone away altogether and grab a book. Now imagine asking yourself that question for a month, "How can I help myself today, what do I need?" and giving yourself exactly that. Try doing that for three months, six months, a year. How much would your life change? Day to day, you might not notice much difference, but the difference a year from now will be huge. Again, it's not always about wanting to make big changes in your life. Maybe it's just the little things. You can also achieve those smaller tasks, by checking in with yourself daily: what change do I want to make today? And those little steps, every day, also help you achieve the big changes that might seem impossible right now. To embrace change you have to create new patterns for yourself that will help you achieve your goals. You have so much potential to change your current situation, and you'll be amazed at how quickly you start to notice those positive changes when you commit yourself to it. You can achieve anything you want if you believe it is possible.

A key factor in creating that change? New patterns. By now we've talked extensively about all sorts of unhelpful things. From unhealthy coping to trauma and labels. But what kind of behavior do we want to replace them with? The trick, of course, is not only to shake off all kinds of unhelpful thoughts, feelings and behavioral patterns, but also to create new ones that are actually helpful. And to repeat those patterns of good behavior over and over, until they become habits that you do every day without even thinking about it. Without new patterns there is no change. Patterns are like water; they choose the path of least resistance. And if you have done something one way a thousand times, you'll probably do it the same way the 1001st time. To break this pattern you have to live more consciously in the moment and ask yourself again and again: what do I want to achieve here? Does this fit with who I really am? What is another way to achieve what I want, that is better for me and fits better with who I want to be?

Suppose you are a real people pleaser. You need others to like you, you are afraid of being rejected, you tend to avoid conflicts and you undoubtedly find yourself regularly doing things simply because you want to be nice or because you are afraid to say no. Of course, you can think, "Okay, I don't want to do that anymore, so the solution is simple: from now on I am going to clearly state my boundaries." Then you find yourself in a situation where you have to do exactly that, state your boundaries. A colleague asks if you can just finish a report, while you are already swamped with work. You think no, yet you sheepishly say "sure." Even though you've decided that you really no longer wanted this pleaser behavior. For you this behavior is second nature, so much so that you will really have to work on a new strategy, otherwise you will continue to behave as you always did. Take another look at your unhelpful patterns. What kind of obstacles do you run into again and again? In doing so, it's important that you realize, "hey, I have to stop pleasing everyone, otherwise people won't get to know the real me. If I say yes and amen to everything, people will never know who

I am and what I want. And, they will step all over my boundaries because, well, I never told them I had any." So, the first and most important step is always to understand *why* you need to break a pattern. Once you know that, you have a goal; you know how much your life will improve when you leave this behavior behind. The next step is understanding when you fall into the pattern. What situations trigger it and what do you feel? For example: "When I get into a situation that... I regularly lapse into the pattern that...' 'I get triggered by.... and this causes me to..." The trick is to start recognizing the pattern. You may not recognize these situations immediately, but suddenly you'll begin to notice, "hey, wait a minute, I'm saying yes even though I want to say no." Be aware of your behavior, and you will see that you start noticing things earlier and earlier. The next step is to actually change it. "Wait a minute, I'm falling into my old pattern, I don't want to do this anymore. This is not going to help me in the long run." Once you recognize this, it's time to stop perpetuating this pattern. That's a conscious choice. You know you are doing it AND you want to change it: so do it. Choose a different path. In the beginning it will feel annoying, scary or unnatural, but this is the only way to break patterns and become the person you really want to be. By consciously choosing different behaviors and breaking old patterns, you slowly carve a small stream next to that big river. Each time you

Old patterns got you where you are today. New patterns will get you to where you want to be.

choose to handle something in a different way, that stream becomes a little deeper. Soon you will start to notice that the water naturally wants to go that way, because you have created a new path. That's how you create new thoughts, new emotions, new behaviors, and therefore new patterns. You can't just do it by thinking about who you don't want to be, but by being exactly who you do want to be.

Being who you are means adapting to change, by breaking old patterns and embracing new ones. Be aware of this and regularly ask yourself: 'why am I doing this, what do I want to achieve? Is there another way to approach this that works better for me and my relationships in the long run? How can I be myself in a way that suits me?' A lot of these patterns are your old self. Again, you can choose who you want to be. All you have to do is to be much more conscious of your thoughts, emotions and actions. Don't run around all day like a headless chicken on autopilot, but really think for yourself! When you start to think more consciously about your behavior, you will see that your environment automatically begins to change to fit with the new life you've chosen. Because you choose healthier patterns for yourself, you will also make better choices when it comes to the people around you. You will see and feel more clearly what it is like to have healthy relationships with people and undoubtedly you'll want to cultivate those kinds of relationships in your life. Because the fact is, just because you work on yourself doesn't mean that everyone around you has also done that work. You are going to meet people who can only see you for who you once were, but you are also going to meet people who fit perfectly with who you are now. This is why growth and change often involves saying goodbye. To parts of yourself, and to others. Once you know and love yourself through and through, you will only want people around you who also have your best interests at heart.

SELF-LOVE

'How could I be so stupid? Pfff, I look so fat! Why am I so clumsy? My nose is so ugly. I can never act normal! I really am a terrible person for letting this happen. I failed again, I'm such a loser. No wonder I wasn't invited, I wouldn't want to hang out with me either

The easiest way to make your life difficult is to be your own worst enemy. We all know that bullying is wrong, and yet we bully ourselves daily. We focus on what we didn't do well, can't do well or even make things up entirely, just to be able to put ourselves down. And your achievements and strengths? You conveniently ignore and trivialize them. After all, it was nothing, you could have done much better. Someone else thinks you're great? Well, that's only because they haven't seen all the bad things yet! Many people will recognize themselves in this kind of self-talk and then also report feeling insecure. Is that really a surprise? No one is going to feel self-confident when they are constantly being belittled like this. If you talked to your friends like that wouldn't they feel the same way? What's more, you wouldn't have any friends left. If you were to make these kinds of statements towards your friends, they would start avoiding you in no time. The trouble is you can't run away from yourself. And because of that, self-criticism is one of the biggest obstacles to staying true to yourself and living life the way you want. Fortunately, there is a solution: self-love.

Before we discuss self-love again, it is important that you are aware of how you are treating yourself right now. Surprise, surprise. Self-criticism, like so much in our lives, is also a learned behavior. Babies are not born with a gene for self-criticism. When a one-year-old falls down taking their first steps, they don't think "oh I can't manage to walk right away, let's never try that again, I'm too stupid to for this." A two-year-old doesn't think "my butt looks so big in this diaper, I'll skip breakfast tomorrow." No, we think this way because we have stored up all kinds of critical comments in our lives, whether they came from a teacher at school, your friends, your parents or even from yourself. And we have subsequently come to believe those critical voices, especially when we have a sensitive nature. Maybe when you were younger, or even in a later phase of your life, you received a lot of criticism from a partner, or maybe a mentor in your workplace. So of course it feels natural to criticize yourself just as harshly. In fact, it may feel like it's something you deserve; after all, you are "too fat, too thin, too loud, too timid, too hyper, too lazy or too stupid." Because of your past, your traumas, the conditions people have placed on love and other difficult experiences, we often find it much easier to be highly critical of ourselves, instead of being there with support, kind words, a big hug and appropriate pride when we succeed. We sometimes seem to forget how to do that; be kind to ourselves. Instead, we are the first to criticize ourselves. Many times, this is because we have created unrealistic expectations for ourselves. When you measure yourself against an unachievable yardstick, it's not surprising that you fail every time. If you never allow yourself to make mistakes, then you will often feel stupid. If you think you have to instantly perform like an expert on your first attempt, you will always remain a failure. If you think you need to look like a supermodel, who is actually photoshopped, you will always find yourself ugly by comparison. Unrealistic expectations in life create disappointments. Unrealistic expectations about yourself, create a shitstorm of self-criticism. If you look at everything with a critical eye, only noticing the things that are wrong, of course you are always going to find something, because let's face it; nobody is ever perfect.

How can you recognize a lack of self-love? You easily allow yourself to be abused or taken advantage of by others. You constantly neglect your own feelings and needs, because you consider yourself less important than others. Constant self criticism,

So many of us have learned that love is conditional and that has changed us. Learn to give yourself unconditional love and you will become who you really are.

pleasing and perfectionism are all behaviors that get free rein when you lack self-love. Another clue is that you're always preoccupied with the opinions of others. After all, you don't think much of yourself so you let others determine your worth. So, what are you good at? Making decisions that are not in the best interest of your physical or mental health. Making choices that you know are not good for you. So, what does self-love look like? Self-love is saying sweet, kind, and positive things to yourself. Self-love is not letting yourself be taken advantage of. Self-love is forgiving yourself for making mistakes and supporting yourself when you have messed up. Self-love is giving yourself constructive feedback and acknowledging where you can do something better. Self-love is spending time with people who have your best interests at heart. Self-love is daring to be vulnerable and asking for help. Self-love is replacing those negative labels with positive ones. Self-love is also recognizing that there are things you don't like about yourself and thinking of ways to change them. Self-love is healing yourself and creating new patterns. Self-love is embracing change. Self-love is acknowledging and expressing your feelings. Self-love is accepting your imperfections. Self-love is not accepting your own bullshit excuses. Self-love is doing, or not doing things, not because it's easy and you always want to, but because you want the best for yourself in the long term. Self-love is being proud of who you are and what you do. Self-love is arranging your life according to your desires and values, rather than what others expect of you. A high level of self-love will have a huge positive effect on your overall health and your relationships. And 'I'm not only talking about your relationship with yourself here, but also your relationships with other people. People who roll their eyes at the statement "I choose myself" are often not people who have a lot of self-love. If you do, you will understand why it is logical and important to put yourself first. If you cannot lovingly care for yourself, you cannot lovingly care for someone else.

So how do we go from that critical voice to a loving one? The good news is self-love is a skill, and a skill you can develop with practice. You strengthen self-love through small actions of love toward yourself. This doesn't have to mean standing in front of a mirror and shouting to yourself "Hey, beautiful, you are awesome, I love you!" You can do it if you really want to, but it's not mandatory. Self-love is buying yourself flowers. Canceling an appointment because you need a rest. Unfollowing people on social media who make you feel insecure. It's not taking a bath and putting on some nice makeup, but having the courage to do difficult things because you know it will help you move forward. Having a difficult conversation with your parents, learning to deal with rejection from others. No longer rejecting yourself. Self-love is also being critical of your unrealistic expectations, critical thoughts and unhelpful beliefs. And instead looking at the positive side of things and focusing on your best attributes. Make the effort to consciously look at your strengths, your hard work, the things you have done well and are proud of. If you want to silence your inner critic and ride the wave of self-love, it is important to start catching yourself when you start thinking these cruel thoughts and questioning them. Suppose you catch yourself thinking "I'll never be able to do that, I'm not smart enough for that." Ask yourself the following questions: is that really true, that I'll never succeed? Is that a fact or my opinion? Is this comment helping me? Do I want to think of myself that way? What would I say to my best friend if they made this comment about themselves? And then immediately switch to self-love by talking positively to yourself instead. "Of course I can do it! Maybe I just need to put in some extra time and energy." Or "I'm not stupid, I've just never done this before." Or, in other situations, "I don't need to be perfect all the time, everybody makes mistakes. I can learn from this." The trick is to look at yourself more realistically and with more appreciation and compassion. In the beginning this is difficult, and you will often catch yourself talking with that negative little voice, but soon you will find that voice becoming more neutral, even positive. Self-love is a skill and with practice you will master it. Until it's second nature, and you don't make situations harder, but give yourself that support that you would give others you love.

Just an important reminder: make sure that unrealistic expectations don't affect your self-love. You do not have to love everything about yourself, although of course you can. You don't have to suddenly love the things you don't like about yourself. You don't have to glorify your lesser qualities; you just have to accept them. Learn to love yourself as you are. With your beautiful as well as your less beautiful sides. You have cellulite on your butt, *so what*! You had to switch studies? *Who cares*? You've made mistakes? *Join the club*. Just as you become more flexible when you learn to embrace change, you will also develop more self-love when you learn to embrace yourself. Self-love is accepting yourself. Everything you begin to accept you begin to appreciate more and more. And everything you look at with love and compassion, you are going to love more. To the point where you think, "Yes, I love myself. I love the people who are important in my life and one of those people is me. And I deserve as much love, respect, and appreciation as I give all my loved ones."

If you reject yourself and are insecure about parts of yourself, it is very difficult to go through life with confidence. You can't hate yourself into going to the gym. When you love yourself as you are, you have your best interests at heart and will want to take good care of yourself as well. That very love for yourself is what *will* make you take that gym class. That love for yourself is going to make you think "I'm making the healthy choice for my nutrition." And that love for yourself is also going to cause you to make healthier choices in the people you tolerate around you and the relationships you enter into. Believe me, *you can't hate yourself happy*. Try thinking and acting out of love for yourself and experience what that does to you. So many people do it exactly the other way around: first I must improve myself and then I will be able to love myself! No, that's not how it works. You have to love yourself first and that will give you the confidence and discipline to improve what you want to improve. To do and let go of things more easily. Simply because you love yourself and have your best interests at heart.

Think again about that younger version of yourself and the exercise I gave you in the first chapter where you went back to a moment in your childhood. Now think back to that little girl or boy who suffered from the criticism of others. What words would have given him or her reassurance and pride? What would he or she have liked to hear about himself or herself? What would have given him or her confidence instead of

It's time to take
care of yourself as well as
you would take care of
someone you love.

insecurity? Next, try turning the things you would say to yourself into affirmations. Write down those phrases and start saying them to yourself daily until you believe them. *I love you. It doesn't matter what others think of you, what matters is what you think of yourself. No one is perfect; it's okay to make mistakes. Trying is how you learn. You are amazing just the way you are. I am there for you unconditionally. You can always count on me. You can achieve anything you want. It's okay to rest, you don't always have to be busy.* To give them extra strength, at some point you can choose to write them down and put them in the "I" form. *I love myself exactly as I am. I am strong and smart. I am my own best friend. I deserve to be happy. I am in control of my life and my thoughts. Every day I choose myself.* Affirmations help us reshape our way of thinking. And when we focus our affirmations on self-love, they help us silence our inner critic and become our own biggest fan, supporter, and advocate. Just think about how you feel when someone says kind, supportive words to you. It immediately gives you a boost of self-confidence, doesn't it? When you start using affirmations, you can achieve that effect yourself.

Why is self-love so important if you want to be yourself? How do you think you can be yourself if you hate yourself and disapprove of everything you do, think, feel, and express? When does a friend or relative feel comfortable enough to be themselves with you? To be vulnerable and show the most beautiful and ugly sides of themselves? It only happens when you give unconditional love and make someone feel good just the way they are. Only then will that person dare to make changes and become his or her authentic self. If you want to be yourself, then you will have to give yourself that same trust. Unconditionally. Even if you are not yet where you want to be. Change begins, as you know by now, with accepting where you are now. Being proud of where you are now. From there, you can start building your ideal future because you know your worth.

OK, so #SELFLOVE is not putting on a mask, throwing a bath bomb in your tub and thinking it will all work out after that. It is catching yourself being cruel to yourself and putting a positive voice in its place. It is asking yourself more often what you need and giving yourself that. Always start your day with the question: how can I help myself today? What do I need? Give yourself that. It is also asking yourself every day: what did I do today that I am proud of? And then naming at least one thing every day. If that happens to be putting on that mask that day, that's totally fine. Self-love is putting yourself first, recognizing what you need and giving it to yourself. Loving the person you already are, so that you will only be yourself more and more.

TRUSTING YOUR INNER VOICE

I f, at this moment and after everything you have read, you think, "yes, I have stayed pretty much true to myself and I am living life the way I want to," then that is confirmation that you have listened to your inner voice. Maybe quite consciously because you hear it clearly. Perhaps unconsciously, it is more of a whisper, but you still feel that you trust yourself in the decisions you make and the way you shape your life. If, on the other hand, you are now thinking "I've lost quite a bit of myself and I've drifted away from the things that energize me," that is confirmation that you probably haven't heard your inner voice for a long time or have pretty successfully ignored it. And it's not that surprising. By now it's not hard to imagine that we learn to listen to a lot of voices in our lives, except for our own. We all experience so much pressure from the world around us and the daily dose of opinions, expectations and tasks, that it can be damn hard to experience the peace of mind that you need to hear that voice. Maybe you are currently experiencing whatever is going on in your head as something more like a crowded pub where everyone is shouting at each other. Or you have a little monkey sitting on your shoulder, banging cymbals and making you walk around with a continuous ringing in your ears. My inner voice? I don't know what that is.

The most helpful thing to do is to look at your past. Have you ever heard your inner voice? And perhaps even ignored it completely? That person you met who you immediately had a bad gut feeling about, but which you ignored, and then that friendship ended in tragedy? That business deal you made that didn't feel right and ultimately turned out not to be that great. That time you were somewhere and experienced an uncomfortable feeling and then, sure enough, something bad happened? That's your intuition trying to talk to you. Our inner voice wants to tell us all kinds of things, if only we can create a little more silence so we can listen to it better. Be aware of the ways this voice has tried to speak to you in the past and think back to the times when you could have listened better, instead of explaining away your feelings with the rational part of your mind. Because that's what often happens. We think "I shouldn't get so worked up, it must be nothing, that's really so illogical, I trust what the other person is telling me."

We have become so accustomed to looking to others when we have questions. If you want to develop your inner voice, try asking yourself the question first. So instead of asking "What do you think about this?"

ask "What do I want? What do I think about this? How do I want to deal with this?" If you start asking yourself better questions more often, you will be amazed at how many good answers you have. Sure, if you want to know what the eighteenth decimal point of Pi is, it's better to just ask google. But all those life questions, which are about you and your life? What do I want from my job? What do I want from that relationship? Or with that friendship? Do I need to do that? How do I deal with my health? That's about you! In the end, you know best how to navigate your unique path. Moreover, you have to live with the consequences of your decisions, so it makes a lot of sense to have your own say. To tune into your voice, ask yourself more often "what do I want or how do I feel about this?" And not just once, but three times in a row. What do I really want? But what do I *really want*? Is that really what I want? Your deeper motivation and wisdom will find breathing room and your inner voice will feel called to have its say.

We have often become so over-rational that we have stopped trusting ourselves when we cannot rationally reason something out. That inner voice is there, but often we just ignore it, doubt it, or quickly look to others to give us the answer. Especially when that inner voice tells us things we'd rather not hear or that may not seem logical yet. For example, that

You don't need to ask
others what you already know deep
down inside. Learn to listen.

this relationship is not good for you. "Why not? He messages me six hundred times a day, especially when I'm away with my girlfriends." That your job, which perfectly matches your years of study, doesn't suit you at all? "But that can't be, when I was seventeen, I was sure this is what I wanted to be!" That this marriage really doesn't make you happy? You imagined it all so beautifully. That this friendship is not good for you? "Hmm, maybe it is a little weird that every time we spend time together, I walk out the door uncertain and doubting everything and everyone." When your inner voice works the right way, it tells you not what you want to hear, but what you *need* to hear. Whether you think that's logical advice or not. The good news: You don't have to act right away. Your voice initially just wants to be acknowledged and heard. It wants confirmation that you understand what's really going on. What choice you make next is only the next step. When it comes to bigger things, you don't need to be hasty. But let's be honest: afterwards how often do you think "I felt for a long time that this would be best for me" or "actually, I knew for a long time that this would not work." See, you can hear it! Sometimes we just prefer to put in earplugs. Remember: many of us would rather be comfortably unhappy than take the uncomfortable road to happiness.

The art of beginning to hear your own voice more and more is about learning to tune out the noise around you. That's what you've been doing throughout the past few chapters. No more letting that trauma chatter in your ears, no more of those labels, no more of those conditions of worth, no more of those negative thoughts or inner critics. The more you can still yourself and let all those negative thoughts pass, the better you can hear yourself. The better you hear yourself, the better you will know yourself. The nicer, sweeter and more valuable you find yourself, the more you will want to listen to yourself. Frankly, it may seem easier to seek answers outside of yourself, but with a little patience, trust, and good listening skills, you will be able to tune into your inner voice for guidance when you need it most.

So how do you recognize the difference between someone else's voice and your own? And how do you recognize the difference between your inner voice and your inner critic? Your inner voice is a calm, gentle voice that is there to guide you in life. It helps you while making choices. It is the intelligent and friendly sister of the nagging, repetitive, negative, critical voice that blares in your ears nonstop. At least for now, because everything you now know about yourself will soon make that a thing of the past. Your inner voice is like your innate intelligence. The one that often knows exactly what is best for you and suits you. It's the most powerful GPS you can have to guide you through life and its choices. It's custom made for you. And yet we often prefer to grab someone else's map from 1964. Quite illogical, isn't it? Your inner voice should weigh more heavily than any other voice. That voice knows you best and has been following you all your life. It is the wise part of you that can soar high above the details of the moment, your own emotions, and the emotions of others to form the best judgment of the situation. After all, the best way to go about something is not something objective, but just whatever suits you best.

There is nothing more powerful than trusting in yourself and fully walking your own path. Your inner voice is your greatest support and guide on your most authentic path. Once you begin to hear it, trust it and follow it, extraordinary things happen. Finding true love, your greatest passion, a great job, a precious friendship. Daring to listen to the advice it gives will bring so much beauty into your life. If there is one tool for knowing, being and choosing yourself, it is to follow your inner voice. It knows the way. Following your inner voice requires courage, because often it is a lot easier to just do what everyone expects of you. Following your inner voice is listening to who you really are and want to be, and making choices that align with that. It means

Always trust your inner voice.
Sometimes it tells you what you want
to hear and it will always tell you
what you need to hear.

that some people will be disappointed because you make different choices than they expected or hoped for. It means that you sometimes have to take risks because the voice is pushing you toward change. It will make you feel like an odd duck at times because you are steering your own course. But following that voice is what you have to do if you want to stay true to yourself and start living your life the way you want.

Oprah once said very aptly, "Trouble arises when you don't pay attention to the whispers of life. Life always whispers to you first, but if you ignore the whispers, sooner or later you'll get a scream." It can be challenging to listen to your inner wisdom, despite all the external noise and internal clamor, but when you start doing it, you will never want to do anything else So, if you don't want to hear your inner voice for now, it is very important to do the following things: be a perfectionist, let your inner critic chatter in your ear all day, jump from one relationship to the next, question yourself, rationalize everything, please people, work hard, always be busy and live on autopilot. Interested in working together with the best GPS out there to find the path to your happy life, though? Engage in some form of exercise, practice mindfulness, go meditate, start journaling. The more you can quiet yourself and give space to your inner voice, the more it will become your best friend and advisor. The more you tune into it, the better and faster you will make choices and solve problems, and the happier and more meaningful your life will be. Your inner voice knows no other way to live than to simply be true to yourself.

We have no control over many things in life, but we do have control over what choices we make. The more you make choices based on your inner voice, the more authentic and therefore happier your life will be. My intention with this book is to have you discover your own truth and then live in constant awareness of that inner truth. If that's too vague for you: I want you to start being yourself and living your most authentic life. When you know who you are, you are not so susceptible to other people's ideas about who you should be and what you should be doing.

If you want to stay true to yourself and make choices that are in line with what makes you happy, it is important to know who you are. When you have a clear picture of your personality, feelings, values, and desires, it becomes easier to create a life that fits you well. That process of self-knowledge is one of the most beautiful things you can go through in life, but it is also a process that is sometimes very challenging and not always pleasant. What you may have noticed is that once you start looking at yourself honestly, you also start seeing things you don't like at all about yourself or your life. Often you also have to do things that you don't like at all or even find scary, sad or difficult to get to where you want to be. So keep in mind that knowing and being yourself through and through is a process of trial and error. A process that never stops. The image you have of yourself can change with every new phase or big event in your life. But, if you keep listening to your inner voice, it will tell you what does and does not suit you, so that you can adjust your life accordingly. It will make you see and dare to make choices that fit who you are, who you want to be and where you want to go with your life. *You will always have your own back!*

CHOOSING YOURSELF

Choosing yourself is not just
about saying yes to yourself. It is also
learning to say no to the world and
not feeling guilty about it.

HEALTHY SELFISHNESS

If there is one thing we all struggle with at times in life, it is what others think about us. Whether it's our neighbor, a family member or that classmate from fifteen years ago; what do they think of me? What do they think of my accomplishments? The work I do? My relationships? How I live my life? Are they going to think I'm selfish if I say no to this? What will they think if I'm not there? What if I confront him about it, he's probably not going to like that at all. Often, we are so focused on what others think, want or need that we structurally neglect our own opinions, feelings and needs. We only need to ask ourselves one simple question: what does it matter what the other person thinks? What does it matter that this person doesn't like the way I dress? Who cares if someone finds it irritating that I say no to an assignment because I simply don't have the time? Who cares that another person doesn't understand that this man makes me happy? Who cares? And this is not meant in an angry, arrogant, or selfish way, it's simply realistic. Why do I care so much about this other person? Why do I care more about what someone else thinks about something than what I think about it? If they criticize something, does that make them the expert? Are they perfect? Why does someone else get to decide what my worth is? Or how I spend my time? Or how I organize my life? That someone thinks a certain way is one thing, they are allowed to have an opinion, but why should I care? Well, you don't have to! You don't have to care what someone else thinks about you or your life. Everyone is entitled to their opinion, sure, and you have the right to completely ignore that opinion and do things exactly the way you want to. Everyone can ask you to do something, and you have the right to deny that request. And what other people think about that? F*ck it.

Socially, the idea of choosing yourself is selfish, and selfishness is still taboo. Being selfish is something to be avoided at all costs. You hear people say things like, "The world is only getting more selfish." But is it? Selfishness is usually seen as having no regard for other people and always putting your own interests above those of others. Are there many selfish people? Sure. Are there also many people who are very altruistic and considerate of others? Absolutely, in fact many more of them. You will find what you are looking for. If you think the world is made up of selfish people, you'll meet them all. If you tell yourself that thinking of yourself and choosing for yourself is selfish, you will experience it that way. Calling you selfish is a way to manipulate you into doing or not doing things for someone else, to structurally put someone else's interests above your own. To keep you running errands for people who often don't do the same for you. It's often the people who think it's selfish for you to choose for yourself who take advantage of the fact that you never do. "Choosing yourself?! But wait a minute, then I have to get out of my comfort zone, I don't feel like doing that!" No, they would rather benefit from your people pleasing behavior. The fact that this is only to their advantage and at your expense, that's not their problem. So, who exactly is being selfish?

Let's agree once and for all that selfishness is, to some extent, very healthy. It is a form of self-protection that has nothing to do with thinking you are fantastic – although you certainly can – but has everything to do with loving yourself in a healthy way. It means loving yourself enough to respect and protect your own energy, time and attention. Healthy selfishness makes you give yourself at least the same respect and attention as those around you. It means that you consider your own opinion about something at least as important as someone else's. Choosing for yourself is not just about saying "yes" to yourself. It is learning to say no to people and things that only cause you stress, without feeling guilty about it. Healthy selfishness is understanding that people may think or expect certain things, but that you get to decide what to do with those expectations.

It's okay to realize that your best friend was a better match for you when you were both in kindergarten. It's okay to hate the job you worked so hard for. It's okay to fall out of love with someone you thought you couldn't live without. It's okay to find out that something you once were passionate about is no longer your thing, and that the things that once mattered to you now don't. It's okay to find out that what you thought would make you happy doesn't, and it's okay to make a change. Today you are someone else than you were 10 years ago. You lived, you learned. It's okay to outgrow the life you once wanted and it is never too late to create a life that is true to yourself.

"But I need so much from myself too, how do I even start?" One step at a time. If you feel overstimulated with everything that is expected of you – or what you *think* is expected of you – start by shifting your *to do's*. Divide them into the categories of "what do I have to do, what do I want to do and what do others want me to do." The tasks that really need to get done; those come first. Because yes, life is not always fun and choosing yourself does not mean you can do whatever you feel like doing 24/7/365. You have obligations, we all do, but we often create many more than we really have. Often our *to-do's* are a mix of things that really have to be done and things that other people or society expect from us, or even that we expect from ourselves, but which are not a must. So, they are things that you can choose whether to do or not to do. Tasks, in other words, where you can make a healthy, selfish choice.

Choosing yourself in life also means choosing yourself in the day that lies ahead of you. Break down your to-do list for your day using the following questions:

What do I need to do?
What do I want to do?
What do others want me to do?

The first list needs to get done, so that gets checked off first. So that's not something like "I have to have tea with that colleague" but "I have to do some grocery shopping, otherwise we won't have anything to eat tonight" or "I have to file my tax return today, otherwise I'll be late and get a fine." Then you start looking at the things that may not necessarily have to be done immediately but that you do want to do. For example, getting groceries for Grandpa and Grandma, because they can't get around so easily anymore and I want to help them out by doing that. Maybe I can even cook for them? So, I can balance doing something for myself and doing something for the people I care about. And then, there is category three: what do others want me to do? All the things that you don't necessarily have to do, and you don't intrinsically want to do, so these are to do's that come primarily from others. Those are the things you should look at with a hyper-critical eye from now on. You can postpone these to the next day or maybe even take them off your list altogether. The block party? I just don't feel like it and who cares if that one neighbor thinks it's dumb that I'm not there? That request to be class mom? That is so not me, and I just can't pull it off right now with all the hustle and bustle of work and family life. I'm not going to do it. I will sign up for some other activities, but I'm not doing this one. That assignment that barely pays off and that I don't really have time for? No is the answer. If it doesn't need to be done, you don't want to do it and it's just something others expect from you? You choose what to do. Choose yourself.

Healthy selfishness is prioritizing yourself and the people closest to you. It is using your time and energy to support yourself and the people you care about most. It is guarding your own health, both physical and mental, and that requires boundaries. Having boundaries does not mean that you don't allow anyone in. It means that you structure your life so that your concern for others does not come at your own expense. It means being open to others, but also daring to say no when necessary. Having boundaries and enforcing them is communicating what you are okay with and what you are not okay with. It is having self-respect and not letting people take advantage of you. It is making self-care a priority. It is making the choice to take a step back and recharge. It is giving yourself permission to do things for yourself and enjoy them, even though they might be of zero benefit to others and just for you. And maybe this is confirmation that you are already doing very well at choosing for yourself. Maybe you are proud of how you handle things; you're confident, generally well balanced and satisfied with your life. Chances are then, that you are someone who prioritizes your own needs sufficiently. That you listen carefully to what you need. Do you notice that you often put your own needs and desires aside for the sake of others? Then this is the perfect opportunity to change that.

It makes perfect sense: are you being selfish when you make your own mental and physical health, and thus your happiness a priority? And then have the energy, love and positivity to contribute to the happiness of others? Or are you selfish when you are running yourself ragged for everyone and are too overstimulated and stressed and fatigued to really be there for others? Because that's the problem with not being able to choose yourself. It's always putting the needs of others above your own. Choosing yourself is not just thinking about yourself, but thinking about yourself in such a way that you can also be there for others in a better way. It's true that choosing yourself will not help some people around you, because they are the ones who benefit from trampling all over your boundaries. But the people who are important to you and who really want you to feel good and be happy, will only encourage it. You can be a happier, more attentive parent when you take good care of yourself. Friends have a happier, more present and supportive friend when you take good care of yourself. A boss has a happier, more productive employee when you take good care of yourself. And you feel so much more energetic, balanced, confident, and happy when you take good care of yourself. In short, choosing yourself in the right way is what's best for everyone.

Healthy selfishness is not only about who and what we spend our energy on, but also about what kind of energy we have as we move through our days and our lives. So often we let how we feel depend on our circumstances. On the weather, the position of the stars, on how a conversation went, that family member who always has something to nag about, what's going on in the news today, how someone reacted to us in traffic. Far too often our energy is reactive. *I didn't sleep well, so I feel lousy today. I got a cancellation, so I feel bad. There has been another natural disaster, I worry so much. I'm late, so my day is already ruined.* If you let external factors constantly determine your mood, your life will become a lot more stressful than you want. Choose the energy you bring to your daily life. Don't constantly let it be dependent on other people and situations. No matter what happens in the world; you determine what energy you bring into your day. This is not selfish; in fact, it helps the world move forward. Misery in the world arises because people are unhappy, jealous, greedy or selfish. Our collective consciousness has to be raised. If you tune into the frequency of love and kindness every day, you are going to create that world around you. You determine what emotion you start your day with and how you deal with things. We have to learn not to *reason* how we feel based on what we see around us: "Oh, I see terrible news, so I feel bad. Oh, it's crowded, so I feel overstimulated." Try turning it around. Look inward and determine how you *want* to feel. How do you want to be in life? What emotions do you want to experience? And if you think, how crazy, realize this: our imaginations can create anything. If we visualize something in our head or call up a feeling in our body, our brain cannot distinguish whether it is our imagination or reality. Try this. Imagine, really imagine, that you cut open a juicy lemon, put it in your mouth and take a big bite out of it; what happens? Exactly, you probably feel your salivary glands producing spit and notice your lips squeezing together at the idea of the sour taste. But are you eating a lemon? No. Do you feel like you are eating a lemon? Yes. That is the power that your thoughts have. Something doesn't have to really happen for you to experience it. And that is why it's so important to determine for yourself, in your mind and imagination, how you approach your day. Not reactively, but actively. Increasingly science shows us that what you imagine, you become and you experience. That is exactly what you attract into your life.

The famous American writer and psychotherapist Wayne Dyer used to say: "As you think, so shall you be." So be selfish in the energy you choose. Make sure you come from a place of love and kindness so that you attract more of that into your life. Don't let it depend on others, choose yourself. A good way to start every day with positive energy is to think: "I am who I want to be, and all my desires are already fulfilled." In the first part of this book you decided who you want to be and what your future looks like. You probably did that because that person and those desires make you happy, make you feel confident and give you peace of mind. The quickest way to achieve this exact thing, to attract it into your life, is to behave as if it is already so. To be this way and feel this way, as if it is already this way. Stick all those positive labels on yourself and use them to feed your self-belief. *I am confident. I am strong. I am social. I am successful. I clearly state my boundaries. I am beautiful just the way I am. I am allowed to be who I am.* Also, use affirmations to express your goals as if you have already achieved them. *I am so grateful for the financial security I get to experience. I am grateful for the love I get to receive in my life. I am grateful for the place I get to live. I am so grateful for the happiness I get to experience.* All those affirmations, through repetition, start to manifest in your life. Your brain does not distinguish between imagination and reality. It believes what you tell it and make it feel. Thinking, feeling, and acting as if everything you want to be and want to make happen is already reality, gives you a sense of accomplishment, relief

You will not always be
a priority to others which is
why it is so important to make
yourself a priority.

and happiness. Instead of starting each day with negativity, frustration, and insecurity that "it's not there" and therefore experiencing a sense that something is lacking, you can also feel as if it's just all already there. Whoever you want to be; be it, until you truly become it. Whatever you want; experience it until it is there. Expressing gratitude daily for all that you are and all that you have, totally changes your life. From that mindset, you can make powerful decisions that align with who you are and where you want to be. And as a result, it becomes your reality. Call it manifesting, call it the law of attraction, quantum mechanics, mumbo jumbo or science. What I know is that it works. Instead of seeing is believing, it's believe first, then see.

If there is anything you're allowed to be selfish about, it is in the thoughts you allow into your head. Worrying about thoughts like "I can't do this," "I'm so insecure," "What if I'm left alone?" or "Suppose I don't succeed?" is praying that exactly that will happen. Again, your head doesn't know the difference between your imagination and reality. Your brain creates what you imagine. When do you think you will give a better presentation? When you tell yourself ten times in a row "I'm so bad at giving presentations, this probably won't go well. I'll probably trip over my words and my face will go red as a beet!" Or when you tell yourself, "I've prepared myself well and I know what I'm talking about. I'm sure I'm going to succeed in getting the story across. I'm going to confidently give this presentation." Of course, research shows time after time after time: what you tell yourself, what you imagine yourself doing, that's going to manifest in real life. So, either you make it virtually impossible for yourself to be who you want to be and live life the way you want to, or you help yourself, by enthusiastically, day after day, telling yourself that everything is exactly as it should be, until the moment you realize that it actually is. Being who you want to be, living life how you want to live it, you don't do that by just hoping for it. You do that by making the decision that it is so. And behaving that way until all the parts of your life fall into place. Healthy selfishness is choosing your own energy, choosing your own persona, choosing your own desires and dreams and already living that way today.

Deep connections with others are essential for a healthy and happy life and a more beautiful world. And for that very reason, healthy selfishness is something we should accept, normalize, and fully embrace. We all benefit enormously from it. The better we take care of ourselves, the better we can take care of others. And the happier we are, the more we can contribute to the happiness of everyone around us.

BEING YOUR OWN BEST FRIEND

If I were to ask you who your best friend is, how long would it take before you named yourself? Being a good friend to another person comes naturally, but doing it for ourselves? Not really. Usually, we try very hard to be unkind to ourselves. We try to escape from ourselves and our thoughts and avoid our feelings by cramming our schedules with appointments, working extremely hard, and eating or drinking too much. Being alone with our thoughts and emotions? *No thank you.* Many of us find being alone difficult, because we are often a very different person with ourselves than with our best friend, sister, father or partner. Would you want to deal with someone who is mean to you all the time? Of course not! So, it's only logical that you would avoid being alone with yourself. To start enjoying your own company more, it's important to become your own best friend. But how can you build a better, stronger, and more loving relationship with yourself? By applying the key qualities that apply to a good friendship to your relationship with yourself as well.

Best friends? They know each other through and through. They are curious about each other and maintain that interest throughout the years. They want to know everything about each other, remain interested and like to check in on each other. They want to get to know each other better and better, so they like to spend a lot of time together. A good friend is the one who asks you how you are really doing; that friend that knows you better than anyone else. What would it be like if you had that same attentiveness towards yourself? How much would you learn about yourself if you looked at your day and life with that same curiosity? How much easier would your life become if you knew yourself inside out? Always stay interested in your own ups and downs.

Best friends? They love each other unconditionally, talk lovingly to each other and support each other through thick and thin. Best friends love you at the times when you are at your best, but also when you are at your worst. They love you despite, or often because of, your imperfections. You messed something up. You're having a bad day? Your best friend looks at what you did well, tells you what they are proud of, or takes the time to sit with you when everything feels like crap. A best friend shows their love by offering a listening ear, by motivating you, helping you or just giving you a big hug. You cannot be your own best friend without that same form of unconditional self-love. The inner critic is a thing of the past. Love yourself and support yourself with the love, words, and actions that a best friend would use. A best friend brings out the best in you and is always your biggest fan, and that's what you are going to do for yourself.

Best friends? They give each other good advice that really helps. If you are struggling with fears, doubts, or an issue where you could use someone's help, your best friend will volunteer with the best of intentions. That person knows you best of all and will help you deal with it in a way that is ultimately best for you. Who knows you even better than your best friend and can give even better advice? You do. Need advice? Listen to your inner voice.

Best friends also respect each other enough to be honest with each other. They don't dick around when there are things you need to hear and will always tell you what you need to hear with good intentions and in a respectful manner. Even when they know you don't want to hear it. But you also don't take it the wrong way because you know they mean well. You are mature enough to receive feedback; you are open to it and learn from it. Being your own best friend means being honest with yourself. All those excuses and nonsense, doing things that are ultimately not in your best interest? Not anymore. You have to speak honestly and respectfully to yourself about those subjects because you want to live your best life.

Everything you
lose by being yourself
didn't belong to you
in the first place.

And you know what best friends also do? Have a lot of fun together! Our friends make life more fun. They know what makes you happy and will do exactly that with you. What else? There is plenty of laughter. About other people, about each other, about life. Being your own best friend means having fun with yourself, spending quality time with yourself and not taking yourself and your life too seriously.

Best friends take care of each other. When you ask them for help, they help. In fact, even if you don't ask for anything, they will often notice you could use some help. When you are sick, they bring you a meal so you can rest, when you are moving, they lift boxes. Best friends ask each other "what do you need?" and give that to each other. Being your own best friend is always taking good care of yourself. Asking yourself every day "what do I need?" and giving yourself that. Not "stop whining, just push through, you have to be able to do it on your own," but "take a break now, I understand you're tired, get some help."

The last thing that best friends always do? They make time for each other. No matter how busy they are, friendship is a priority for them, so they will always try to spend time with each other. If you are your own best friend, that time with yourself is just as important. Don't do everything else first and then see what is left for yourself at the end of the week. No, grab your calendar at the beginning of the week and put big X's in the places where you will make time for yourself. In most phases of your life that time does not appear out of nowhere, you have to take it.

To be your own best friend is to take good care of yourself; mentally, physically, emotionally, and spiritually. This is a choice you make every day. Being your own best friend makes it easier to choose yourself. And choosing yourself makes it easy to always act like your own best friend. You create a very healthy, helpful feedback loop for yourself. Certain rituals help us tremendously to strengthen and deepen the bond we have with ourselves. We know these rituals best these days as #selfcare. Magazines and the Internet are full of them and there is an entire industry devoted to them. And because it revolves almost entirely around products, we tend to think "if I put on a facemask – especially if it's from brand X – I'm taking good care of myself." But true self-care goes much further. Take care of yourself. And not just superficially, by putting two slices of cucumber on your eyes and thinking that your mental breakdown will subside, no, go deeper. It's about thinking, what do I really need? And giving yourself that. It is not making vague plans with yourself, but establishing routines and keeping the promises you make with yourself. So, it's not "I need to take good care of myself," but "I'm going to take good care of myself by journaling for five minutes every morning when I wake up and every night before I go to sleep and in doing so work on gaining more self-confidence and balance." It's not "I'll cram my calendar full of appointments and see if there's anything left for myself at the end of the day or week," but rather scheduling that time in your calendar at the beginning of the week and consciously making it specific. Figure out what you need at that moment. Because self-care means checking in with yourself: what do I need? Rest? Social contact? A phone-free evening? A gym buddy? An evening of Netflix and a pint of ice cream? Nothing is more unfortunate than spending the time you have to yourself scrolling mindlessly on social media, only over-stimulating your brain more. What do you really need? How can you more consciously use your time for something you really need? Which form of self-care suits you best depends entirely on who you are. Selfcare for an extrovert might be time with a group of friends or participating in a team sport to recharge your social battery. Self-care for an introvert might be taking time every night to read a book or practicing yoga. Make sure you are open to trying different things. Maybe reading is not for you, but you really love meditation. How often do you really think about what energizes you and whether you make enough time for that? What made you really happy as a child?

Is that something you can bring back into your life, in a different way perhaps? Being your own best friend is being very aware of what exactly makes you happy and what recharges your battery. It's about knowing what calms your mind and doing more of that. It's understanding your own needs and meeting them. Not forgetting yourself and not feeling guilty when you take time for yourself. Self-care is an important part of having a good relationship with yourself. It makes you feel calmer, more decisive, more balanced, and more confident. Being your own best friend helps you make the right choices for yourself and gives you the peace of mind to keep doing that repeatedly, in words as well as in actions.

Now suppose you find it difficult to be your own best friend. To align the values of a good friendship with the relationship you have with yourself. To keep the right thoughts in your head or to take the right actions. To really find that space for yourself. What can help is to choose a fictional person as your best friend. This could be anyone, but what often helps is to choose someone you look up to. Suppose you are a huge fan of a particular athlete, singer, expert, or maybe a wise relative who is no longer alive. It could be anyone you hold in high regard. When you need advice, you can ask this person. Okay, not literally, but figuratively. What would Nelson Mandela do right now? How would Beyonce handle this? What advice would Oprah give me? Say you're a big fan of Cristiano Ronaldo and you want to get into better shape. At night on the couch, you still want to grab that bag of chips. "Would Ronaldo do that now?" Of course not. He would say "come on now, a deal is a deal, have a little discipline now, tomorrow you will regret it!"' Another example: you want to be a more confident entrepreneur, but you find it difficult to feel powerful. Then you might ask yourself, "Would Kris Jenner doubt herself?" Or more generally, "Would a confident person doubt themselves like that?" If you allow yourself to be advised and supported in your thoughts by someone you hold in high esteem, or if you think, feel and act with the identity of the person who is already what you want to be, it becomes easier to choose for yourself. It helps you to create the right thoughts, feelings, and actions. Always ask yourself: does this behavior help me be the person I want to be? What would ... do in this situation? The trick is to start seeing yourself as the type of person who does what you want to do. I'm the type of person who doesn't care about another person's opinion. I'm the type of person who can resist temptations and has self-discipline. If you know the identity of the person you want to be advised by, or the person you want to be, it becomes easier to behave that way. Suppose you quit smoking, it doesn't help to say "no, I quit, so I don't need a cigarette." It becomes easier if you say, "I don't smoke." You identify as a non-smoker.

It's okay to need time for yourself. It's okay to think about your own needs. It's okay not to be able to offer a helping hand because you need it yourself. It's okay to take a step back and not do anything useful for a while. It's okay to feel stressed about everything on your plate and it's okay to empty that plate. We all need rest and time for ourselves. Don't feel guilty about it. It's time to choose yourself.

You can say "I don't drink anymore" or "I don't drink." The second is an identity. You could think "I'm so excited to take the stage" or think "Adele would be saying *go for it* right now. I wouldn't have gotten anywhere either if I hadn't tried." There is always a way to start thinking, feeling, and acting like your own best friend.

It is SO important for your mental health to give yourself the credit you demand from others. To celebrate your own successes. Too often we wait for affirmation from others to make us feel "worthy" or "successful." But why does someone else have to do that? Why can't we give that to ourselves? After all, you know best what you've had to go through to get where you are. You know better than anyone else that you have been the one who has started each and every day and made the best of it, even on the days when no one realized how tough things were. You do it all. No one else can live life for you. No one else sees the complete picture. You will always continue to seek validation from others if you don't learn to give it to yourself. Because all those voices are no match for the one person you really need to hear from: yourself. Tell yourself how proud you are of everything you have done. Thank yourself for persevering and overcoming the greatest challenges. Pat yourself on the back and tell yourself how grateful you are for all the growth you are going through and how much you love yourself. You are doing great. That's not an opinion, it's a fact. And you are ALWAYS worth it. You can be proud of yourself.

By developing a better relationship with yourself, you also develop the ability to be a better friend, partner, or colleague to others. Giving yourself time and attention makes you feel good, and because you feel good, it also makes it easy to choose for yourself in everyday life. Dependency on others disappears and precisely because of this you can build more stable and healthy relationships with them. Spending time with yourself will get better and better because you are more and more okay with yourself. And before you know it, you will always have your best friend by your side in life.

YOUR RELATIONSHIP
WITH OTHERS

The fact that you are reading this book is going to enrich your life in many areas. Who might not be thrilled about that? Some of the people around you. Just be prepared, it won't be long before you hear someone say "you've changed" or "I didn't expect that from you." And that's exactly when you need to start paying attention. Because such a comment can, of course, come from someone who has your best interests at heart. When they say "you have changed," they mean "how amazing that you know so much better who you are and what you want. That must feel good! I am so proud that you are doing things that I never would have expected! You are really standing up for yourself, you are no longer blowing whichever way the wind goes. I'm really impressed!" But unfortunately, much more often, when you start to heal and grow, the chaff starts to separate from the wheat. Then you start hearing things like "I didn't expect that from you, you have really changed" with a hidden subtext; "I had a certain image of you in my head, but now all of a sudden you are behaving very differently, and I don't like that. I don't like the way you are now at all." It is important to realize that you can reinvent yourself in relationships. Not everyone will find this easy, and it may cause some friction, but that doesn't mean it is wrong for you to change. To what extent are you willing to change yourself to fit into a relationship and to what extent must your relationships change to fit you? That is the central question at play in the relationships you have with others.

Actually relationships are the perfect test case for checking whether you really know, are and choose yourself. Especially in relationships, all the old junk from the past surfaces. The closer you are to someone, the more vulnerable you are and the sooner you will be triggered. If you are very dependent or looking for affirmation, your jealous side will come out. If you've never learned to set boundaries, chances are you're going to start trying to please. You will start looking for appreciation, you will start imagining crazy things and revert to patterns that are like waving a red flag in front of a charging bull. The great thing about relationships: they are the best learning tool for becoming your most authentic self. After all, if you resolve the shit that comes up, you're going to look at your relationships with new eyes. And you may start to see the people around you differently too. Which people do I want to spend my time with? How do I want them to interact with me? Do they still fit with who I am and the person I want to be and how I want to live my life?

Life will regularly send people to you to see if you have really learned your lesson. A lot of people are not your type, they are just your pattern. Oh, you thought you dealt with that trauma? Well, let's see how fast you fall into this guy's arms. Oh, you're not stuck in that dependent pattern anymore? Let's see what happens when exactly that type of person comes into your life. Relationships are the place where all our old pain holds a party. So, it is very important to realize that the more you heal, the more you experience what it is like to feel good, the less you will want to allow negativity and drama in your life. Relationships are the greatest test to see if we can truly leave the past behind, take the lessons learned and make new connections with the version of ourselves we want to be. Relationships will continue to challenge and trigger you, but each time you stay true to yourself, you will see that relationships also amplify your growth tremendously. It's true. Relationships bring out the worst, but also the best in us. Choose your path.

We often find it difficult to balance choosing ourselves and our relationships with the people who are important to us, but the funny thing is, especially in healthy relationships, it's not that complicated at all.

It's okay to let go of relationships
that no longer serve you. Sometimes you
grow together, sometimes you grow apart.
Sometimes friendships cost more than they
yield. Sometimes we drift away from loved
ones, sometimes family relationships become
debilitating and toxic. Setting boundaries
with people who mentally exhaust us or
severing relationships that do us more harm
than good is one of the most important
forms of self-care and self-love.

Those who have your best interests at heart love you just the way you are. They understand that you need space for yourself. That you have your own wants and needs, which they also want to help you satisfy. If you have healthy relationships, with your partner, with your children and with your family members, then there is no reason that you have to put yourself last. If you do, it is your own pattern, and you have to solve it yourself. What is a good relationship for you? And which relationships that you have now – romantic, platonic, with family or colleagues – meet those conditions? It's okay to let go of relationships that no longer serve us. Sometimes you grow together, sometimes you grow apart. Sometimes friendships structurally cost more than we get out of them. Sometimes we drift away from loved ones; sometimes family ties become debilitating and toxic. Setting boundaries with people who exhaust us mentally, or ending relationships that do us more harm than good, is a very important form of self-care and self-love. When you always prioritize your partner, family, friends, or colleagues more than yourself, you automatically put yourself in second place. You teach the people in your relationships that you are below them. Giving love and being there for one another is a wonderful quality, but not if it comes at the expense of yourself every time. Learn to say no and set your boundaries. Setting boundaries may sound negative, but it is actually an important building block in making your relationships closer. When you can properly communicate who you are, what you do and how you want things to be, it becomes much easier for others to read you, understand you and meet your needs. And so, choosing yourself is not just a matter of "just" setting your boundaries and learning to say no. It means understanding why you have always found that so difficult and knowing how you want your life to be. Healthy relationships are built on healthy patterns, in which you always remain true to yourself.

If you are not feeling good about your relationships right now, ask yourself why that is. Why are you sad? Why are you angry? Why are you disappointed? Ask yourself: whose responsibility is it to fix this? Is it on me, because I still have a piece to heal from the past, or is it on the other person? Always being open to your own growth is one of the most beautiful qualities you can have and will enrich your life. But don't be blind to the other person's role. Maybe you feel sad because you don't get along with someone? Or because you always give attention to people who ignore you? Because you constantly make time for someone who is always too busy for you? Or maybe you give too much to people who take you for granted? To choose yourself is to heal and rebuild yourself from the inside out, so that you no longer tolerate this kind of behavior. And yes, that can be very painful and lead to confrontation, because sometimes these are people who are close to you. But eventually you will have to choose yourself and your happiness. Distance or even saying goodbye for good is the only way to solve this.

Michelle Obama had this to say about friendship. When asked if all her friendships had survived her move to the White House and becoming First Lady, she said, "No, not all of them. Lost oxygen, couldn't make the climb." In other words, as you grow or become more successful, you have a growth spurt, but not everyone pulls that off. For some, you have climbed too high, and they will fall somewhere along the way – due to a lack of oxygen. This is precisely why it is also important to stay open to new friendships and people you meet at the level you're at now. And of course, if the people around you now are ready to grow with you, bring them along! But, when they show you who they really are, believe them. If they no longer fit who you are now, take action. Let them go. Let people fade into the background. Don't go trying to prove yourself or hold onto something that no longer works. Respect the fact that some relationships are for life, and some are for a while. Sometimes you grow together to a certain height, sometimes you grow apart. Let that happen. And then look back fondly on the wonderful times you had together, rather than with bitterness that this happened.

The more healed you are, the more unhealed people will withdraw from you. After all, how does a person who loves themself behave? "I have boundaries. I have standards. I have values. I know who I am. I am always myself. I don't change depending on who I'm with." Some people are not going to like that. They've known a different you for so long and they liked the control that they had over you. Your growth is going to be very challenging for them. Not least of all because you are going to show them that change is always possible. And that is exactly why you are going to look at them differently. You feel good, you feel dynamic, you are self-aware, you are open to learning. So, you no longer attract toxic behavior. You no longer accept that negative energy. You won't accept it when people play games with you, when you don't feel good or when people don't support you. You now know what it feels like to choose for yourself and deal with people in a healthy way. Why should you be okay with people who won't give you that respect? It's perfectly normal that some people still need to grow and find their own way. Above all, give them that space. But if you are not ok with the way someone treats you, that is a hard limit. That is the difference between moving along or staying behind. Normally you would doubt yourself in this kind of situation, it would provoke anger or sadness in you, but the healed version of you is much calmer about this. You are able to look at things from a distance and not make someone else's problem your problem. You will think "it is what it is," more often. You'll see much better what is yours to solve or to work on together, and what is someone else's responsibility. Because you know who you are and what you stand for, because you feel good and enjoy your own company, you are able to reach an unprecedented level of self-confidence and inner peace. And you expect other people to treat you as well as you treat yourself.

Authentic people are who they are and do not change with the company they keep or the opinions of those around them. Choosing yourself means always being yourself and never compromising to fit in. In relationships, you have to be sincere and vulnerable, and you have to have the confidence that the other person will handle it appropriately. It is important to set boundaries with family and friends because this improves your relationships. People know where they stand and what they can expect from you. If you behave like a chameleon, changing all the time, you should not blame people for doing what they want. Have you ever indicated what you want? Oh, do you find that people take advantage of you? Have you ever told them that you are not at all okay with their behavior? We often find it difficult to get a "no" across our lips or to indicate a boundary, but then we are disappointed with people when they cross those boundaries. Do you know what the only common denominator is in all those relationships where you are being abused? You! Standing up for yourself is something you must do for other people. By showing your true colors, you also give others the chance to get to know you better and deepen their relationships with you. Setting boundaries is the only way to live authentically. Only when you learn to say no can you filter out the people and situations from your life that try to make someone else out of you. If you must give up your authenticity to keep someone in your life, then you must ask yourself whether you want that person in your life any longer. So, you must start acting as who you are now, not as who you once were. At one time you may have been someone who allowed yourself to be taken advantage of, but that person is no longer you. Look at how that other person is dealing with that and base your follow-up actions on that.

Another thing to remember: friendships are not about quantity, but quality. Whether you see each other weekly, monthly, or yearly is not so important. What matters is that you have people around you that you can build on. Acquaintances, you can have busloads of them. People to have a nice evening with, great! But real friends? There are often a lot fewer of them. These are the people who are there when you are doing well and when you are doing badly. When it really matters, you start to see who is really there for you. For example, when you're deep in the shit, emotionally or financially. Suppose your business is going poorly, you are on the verge of burnout, who is there? Who is there to help you, support you, put your affairs in order, fill up the fridge or go through some paperwork with you? Who can you call at such times and who will come? In those moments you really get to know people.

As a child, you do not get to decide what your environment looks like. It's just there and you have to accept it. But you do have the choice to leave a toxic or negative environment as soon as you are old enough to walk away from it. In your youth you can point your finger at someone else – and rightly so – but in your adult life you must take that responsibility yourself. However difficult that may be, it is your job, not someone else's, to make your environment a fresh, green park full of flowers instead of a forest where fires are constantly raging and all the animals are fleeing in terror. Ask yourself what you really consider important in a good relationship and ask yourself the question: does this relationship meet it? This can sometimes be very hard, for example if you must break off contact with a parent, your bestie, or your partner for this reason, but you really have to dare to choose yourself. If you are in a relationship and the other person is unwilling or unable to grow, you must dare to make choices. You cannot expect to stay true to yourself and live your best life if you continue to surround yourself with people who constantly belittle you and try to pull you down. You cannot change others, so change yourself. That is the only thing that really affects you. See if the other person is open to changing with you, and if not? Accept that and move on. Embrace change in your relationships. It is a natural process. Clinging to something that is no longer going well will only work against you. Let it go. Choose yourself and the people who actually choose you.

To have healthy relationships, you must be realistic. No one is perfect. To make a deep connection with someone, the relationship does not have to be flawless. You have to let each other be free to be who you are. Don't make your expectations too high because only disappointments will follow. The relationships in your life do not all have to give you everything all at once. Different relationships can meet different needs. You may experience a different kind of love for your partner than for your mother, and one friend may be the fun one, while another is there for that dose of sage advice. Everyone's character and role in your life is different and so is your relationship with them. Just as you shouldn't hold yourself to too high a standard, you shouldn't do the same to others. The worst advice you can get about relationships is that a good relationship should not take effort. That's complete nonsense! If you think like that you are only deluding yourself that perfection exists. No matter how much you love someone and how much you are on the same page, there will always be things you don't agree on. There will always be needs that someone can't meet or things you have to hash-out, or else they'll cause friction. There will always be parts of yourselves that either you or the other person has yet to heal. This is also why arguments are not a bad thing and why it is good to discuss your problems openly. If you can discuss things with each other in a respectful way, it provides space to set things right. By starting the conversation – and sometimes it's okay to be tough – you can get from frustration to solutions. By staying true to yourself, being who you are now and communicating clearly about that, you will see that your relationships become even closer. You can use these moments to see how you can love each other even better, whether platonically or romantically. A healthy relationship takes effort and means that you are always changing, because in a healthy relationship there is always room for growth.

Should you dredge up old memories? No! In a healthy relationship it is important to be able to put the past to rest. To draw a line under what has happened, but also to say, "Okay, I learned my lesson from it, from now on we will deal with each other differently." If you want to continue having a loving relationship, there is no point in continuing to pour salt on old wounds. It makes no sense in a parent-child relationship to keep poking at bruises from the past. Learn to apologize or forgive if you want to move on. The only other option is to say goodbye. You wouldn't want to get stuck in an endless conflict with yourself, so don't do so with others. Allow yourself more than that. Look further and determine what you expect from yourself and from others. What your limits are and what you do and do not accept. The fact that a relationship is rocky does not mean that it cannot be repaired. However, this requires growth on both sides. Acknowledge mistakes, learn from them and find a new way of dealing with each other that meets the basis you find important in a loving and respectful relationship.

There will always be people who want to pull you down. Make sure those people are not in your inner circle. You become who you hang out with. If you want to be the best version of yourself, you cannot surround yourself with people who prefer to see you at your worst. Or who don't have the ability to grow themselves and prefer to pull you down to their level. Those people are not part of the inner circle. And you don't need to worry about what they do. What they think of you or think they know about you? You don't have to care. If you know and choose yourself, you don't care at all about the opinions and expectations of people who are in that outer circle of acquaintances. What those people think of you is none of your business. You are your own best friend; you have the right people around you and that's all you need. Don't make yourself feel good by getting applause from that outer circle, and then it won't affect you when they start spewing negativity again.

In relationships, whether they are friendships, business partnerships, family, or romantic partners, ask yourself: what do I really want? What do I need? Am I my own best friend if I behave this way? Or if I accept this behavior? It is less about reacting in the moment and more about observing what is really happening. How am I behaving? What is the other person doing? If I take a bird's-eye view of the situation, what do I think about this? Do I need to change a pattern? Can I trace a particular pattern of reaction to my past? When is it my turn and when is the ball in the other person's court? Love, respect, loyalty, these are very important values to have in any relationship. These are qualities you want to give, but you also want to receive in return. If that doesn't happen on both sides, know that you don't currently have your best interests at heart. That something needs to change. Choosing yourself in relationships does not mean making it a one-man

Your relationship with yourself is
your relationship with others. If you want
a better relationship with others you've got
to work on a better relationship with yourself.
Once you start choosing yourself, you'll
also start attracting people around
you who really choose you.

show, but building a solid foundation in which you feel free to be yourself and to live your life the way you want to. Sometimes that means a little giving, sometimes it means a little taking, but when the core of love, respect and loyalty remains intact, it is a relationship that you want to welcome into your life with open arms.

Looking at the bigger picture, relationships are incredibly important in our lives. They provide perspective, which we all need. Contact and touch are important life necessities. So, choosing yourself does not mean saying "I don't need anyone, I'll do it all by myself. If people don't do exactly what I want, *fuck them*, I'll stay alone forever." No matter how well you take care of yourself and how much love you give to yourself, it is in our nature to want to make connections with others. With the world hardening and contacts becoming increasingly superficial, a lack of genuine connections is something that can create many mental health problems. So, invest attention, energy and time in relationships, and choose quality over quantity. Understand that relationships flow in and out of your life to teach you lessons and to help you grow and prosper. There will be people who will stay with you throughout your life and play a special role in your story. There will also be people you may only know for a short time, but with whom you feel a deep connection and wouldn't want to be without.

At the same time, there will also be people who will challenge you to resolve old hurts or become more empowered and then may leave. There will be people who will teach you lessons. They will trigger you until you realize: I am not going to give away my time and energy to this person. Those people are also valuable in your life because they show you what is important to you. Be open to all those forms of relationships; some bring healing, others a lesson. It is up to you to see the difference.

Relationships mirror how we view ourselves. If we think highly of ourselves, love ourselves and know that we are valuable, that also forms the basis of our relationships. There is respect, there is pride, there is support and there is love. If you look around you and you see chaos, criticism, hurt and jealousy, there is work to be done. It starts from the inside out; follow the steps of this book and not only will you be stronger, your relationships will be too. Improve yourself, know what you expect from others, and learn when to throw out the rotten apples. This is exactly why the best relationships – whether with yourself or with others – are those in which you feel free to be yourself and feel supported to live life your way. It is a relationship where love, respect and loyalty always prevail. Never forget: your relationship with yourself, is your relationship with others. If you want a better relationship with others, then work on a better relationship with yourself. Once you start choosing yourself, you also start gathering people around you who really choose you.

BEING IN YOUR POWER

What is the quickest route to stress, insecurity, fears, doubts, and a ticking time-bomb of negativity? Living according to other people's opinions and expectations, chasing dreams that are not your own and letting other people control who you are and what your life looks like, while you keep postponing the things you really want until "someday." Because of everything you have read in this book, you are now doing the exact opposite: you have started to stand in your power. You know who you are, you know how to be yourself, and you know how to choose yourself. You now have in your hands the formula for living authentically.

Knowing yourself + being yourself + choosing yourself = living authentically.

Authentic living is always staying true to yourself and living life the way you want to. The only thing left for you to do, with this knowledge in your pocket, is to stand in your power and DO it. Every single day. And for that you always want to stay focused on the three parts of this formula. You always want to be focused on who you want to be and how you want to live your life. All change and growth begin with awareness. Awareness of your past, your present and your future. Of your strengths and your flaws. Of your desires and dreams. If you want to make choices that make you happier and that really come from your heart, it is important to know what you believe in and what you want. What suits you and what doesn't? What do you want more of and what do you want to let go of more and more? When you know this, you can act accordingly. Next, it is important to make conscious decisions for yourself. Again, you will have to go into action mode here. Not by rushing into things, but by pausing more often before making decisions. By giving yourself morerest. By giving your inner voice space, rather than defaulting to old patterns. Whether it's big decisions, about your work or relationships, or small decisions, like whether you want to go out for drinks downtown. Stop and think about what you *really* want before you spend your time and energy on something you don't feel like doing at all. Ask yourself "do I really want this?" Give yourself space for awareness: are you doing things because you are choosing for yourself or because you are falling into old patterns, such as pleasing behavior? Sometimes you will do things in life that you may not feel like doing right away or that cost time, but also benefit you in the long run. That's fine, of course. However, the idea is not to structurally do things that let you drift away from yourself. So, ask

You don't have to be who
the world thinks you should be. You
have to discover who you really
are and then find the courage
to live your truth.

yourself more often the question "what do I want?" or "what do I need right now?" Or "how do I want to deal with this?" A pause helps you make better decisions. There is a very big difference between consciously choosing to help someone or pleasing them because you're on autopilot. Also, take that same pause when it comes to emotions. When something triggers you, don't react immediately. Press pause and ask yourself "where is this reaction coming from? Do I really want to spend my time and energy on this right now?" You'll be surprised how many things you let go. By using your pause button, you will start to react consciously, and by allowing yourself to properly sense and monitor your boundaries you can live more authentically.

I want to... *change patterns; be more indifferent to others and do what I want; react less quickly, but more consciously; be less strict with myself; live more in the moment and for myself rather than stressing about other people; embrace my past AND my bright future; live more in the moment; be my own best friend; lower the bar and make less high demands on myself; live with trust instead of fear; tell people what I really want and feel; listen to my inner voice; go out of my comfort zone and pursue my dreams; leave this relationship; stand behind my own choices, no matter what anyone else thinks; stop feeling insecure by comparing myself to others; plan better; say goodbye to a friend; let go of having to be successful; follow my dreams without comparing them to others; stress less about being good enough or successful; be more content; stop pleasuring myself; know who I am: get more rest; not feel responsible for other people's shit; live according to my own rhythm instead of society's; accept myself and be proud of who I am.* These are some of the thousands of responses I received when I asked "what would you like to change about your life?" Being in your power means doing this. Not saying "I want." Saying "I will." Not saying "I'll never manage to…" because now you know that's a self-fulfilling prophecy! Instead say "I'm going to make sure that…" Not "I want to… be," but "I am…" Being in your power is the result of knowing who you are and choosing that person. Unconditionally. Even if it might not be pleasant for a while and you start to think "help!" Even then. You choose yourself. Always! Every day you get to make that choice over and over again. Every day you do your best to live by it. Sure, sometimes at the end of the day you will think '"hmm,"' today didn't quite work out. But that's okay. That was your day. Anything that didn't work out today, do it again tomorrow. Leave what is behind you behind. Draw the lesson from it. Then look ahead. You don't control the decisions you've made, only the decisions you're going to make next. And the next day, you wake up and re-establish your power. This is who I am, this is what I want, this is what I choose. Choices determine our lives to a much greater degree than circumstances. In every moment you can choose yourself anew.

Being in your power also means holding yourself accountable for your own nonsense when necessary. Hold yourself accountable for doing what you say you are going to do, so that you can feel proud of yourself and always trust yourself. If you say you're going to choose yourself today by going to the gym at eight 8 am, you don't stay in bed with a silly excuse. You go to the gym at eight o'clock. If you say you are going to help yourself today by saying no to that invitation to that party, then you are not going to agree anyway out of guilt. You'll send a clear message that unfortunately you won't be able to attend and then enjoy the peace and quiet you've created for yourself without guilt. If you say that you are not going to eat chips today because you want to be healthier, then you are not going to lie on the couch at night with that bag of sourcream-and-onion. Keeping promises that you make I to yourself is a choice, and every time you make the choice NOT to put yourself first, it feels like a disappointment. A disappointment in yourself. Self-confidence is not gained or lost by how other people think about you, it's all about how you think about yourself! And that is why you make agreements with yourself, with

If you want to live a happy life you should know when it's time to leave. The party. The argument. The friendship. The job. The relationship. The bullshit. When it's time to go, just go.

the intention of keeping them. And every time you keep them, you'll feel damn good about yourself. Because doing what you promised yourself increases your self-confidence. After all, self-confidence has everything to do with being able to trust yourself. Trusting yourself, always being your own safe haven, that lets you stand in your power.

From now on, stop using your energy to worry, to talk down to yourself, to doubt and fear. Make the conscious choice from now on to use your energy to heal, to trust, to be loving to yourself and others and to manifest your best life. Make choices that align with your happiness, distance yourself or say goodbye to the people and things that do not align with it and say a full-throated YES to yourself. Close the gap between what you want and where you are now. After all, you always have the opportunity to change the way you think about and treat yourself. You are not who someone else thinks you should be, you are not the way you think you are; you are the way you choose to be. You have a choice, in every moment of every day, to act as the person you want to be and shape your life more and more the way you want it to be. Take active control of your life. You have that power of choice.

The greatest challenges of our lives are also often the greatest opportunities to stand in our power and live more authentically. All those small obstacles and big low points may cause discomfort, sadness, stress, or anger, but they also help you achieve and experience new things, something you sometimes don't realize until years later. Be grateful for all the shit that has come your way. It has shaken things up, allowing you to see more clearly what is important to you. It's the perfect way to have that "aha moment" and see that you've been spending too much time and energy on the wrong things because you still had old issues to resolve. And it's the perfect way to regain your focus and value yourself. Life doesn't get easier; you just get wiser and stronger all the time.

An authentic life begins with an authentic day. Every day, with every choice you make, you can stand in your power or give that power away to something or someone else. Whatever stage of life you are in and whatever age you are, there will always be people who influence you to put on a mask or to do things you don't want to do. Sometimes you will be that person yourself. Learn to recognize it and turn it around. Be your own best friend. Believe in yourself, always be true to yourself, motivate yourself and watch yourself grow with empathy. To be in your power is to begin each day with the intention of making today a good day, where you stay true to yourself. Ask yourself, "what can I do today to help myself?" Look for the little things and moments where you can make improvement today. Do those things. Even if it's just one thing. And at the end of the day go to sleep, only to wake up the next morning and ask yourself again "what can I do today to stay true to myself?" Then do it again. It's about doing it, not about doing it perfectly. It's about intention as well as consistency. Because all those small actions build over weeks, months, and years to a life-changing result. To make the changes you want to make in your life, you don't have to suddenly change your whole life. You just need to choose yourself today and repeat that tomorrow.

BETTER QUESTIONS,
BETTER ANSWERS

I f you were me, would you resign? Do you think it's a good idea if I break up with you? Do you have any advice for me on how best to handle things with that friend? Do you think I can do that? How would you handle that co-worker? Maybe you regularly ask someone else for advice. You present a problem and ask what the other person thinks is the best solution. Suppose someone were to ask you the questions above. Would you know the answer? Of course, you can give whatever advice seems best to you. With the emphasis on *what seems best to you.* After all, you reason largely from your position, your character, your values, your desires, and dreams. Even if you know someone very well, you still do not know what's best for that person, because you are still not in his or her shoes. What is best for you may not necessarily be best for someone else. And even if something seems best, it can always turn out differently. The only person who can answer these questions is the person who asks them. When you ask someone for advice about your life, there is only one person who can give you the best advice: yourself. After all, the answer is not black and white.

There is often no "best" way; there are many shades of gray. What you should do depends on the context and situation. It depends on the person you are and what you want with your life. And the only person who can best assess what is useful to do is you. So, the person who can best provide you with advice is yourself. But to do that, you need to start using yourself as an advisor a little more often. Instead of asking others those important questions, or at least instead of only asking others, ask yourself.

I don't understand why she stays with him; I would have left a long time ago. You are capable of much more, why do you settle for that job? You want to build a business, why don't you spend that time with your children? Well, I would never want to live in a place like that, terrible. Why wouldn't you shave your armpits, how gross! Who believes in the power of precious stones, that's just a scam! Huh, are the three of them in a relationship? I don't think that's normal, how could someone want that? Well, that's all right, because you don't have to do it. You don't have to live that way. You can choose not to pursue a career. You don't have to take supplements or wear a crystal around your neck. Go ahead and wax your whole body including your head if you feel like it. And if you want to have sex with the same person for fifty years, do it. Enjoy! The way people live has everything to do with who they are, what they

Rule number one:
always stay true to yourself.

want and what growth they have yet to experience. Where you may find something incomprehensible, it can be normal to someone else, and where you find something very logical, someone else might think "why would you do it that way?" And sometimes we all just don't have a f*cking clue and are just taking a stab in the dark. So many people, so many wishes. And that's exactly why it's so important not to live by other people's expectations, opinions, or advice, but to steer towards your own voice, your own truth and what feels best for you.

Being and living authentically requires asking questions that reveal exactly that: who are you and what do you want? It's not asking the question "what are my parents going to think about this?" but "what do I think about this?" It's not asking yourself "how can I get someone's respect?" but "why am I listening to someone who doesn't respect me?" Not "what is the community going to think of my relationship?" but "what do my partner and I think of our relationship?" Not "how can I find someone who loves me?" but "how can I love myself more?" Not "how can I show that I haven't changed?" but "how do I feel about someone important to me not celebrating my successes?" Not "what was shitty about today?" but "what went right?" Not "why does this have to happen to me?" but "how do I best handle this?" With the right questions, you can shift your focus to a place that has your best interests at heart. A shift from other people's opinions to your own opinion. From unrealistic expectations to realistic ones. From a sense that something is lacking to a sense of gratitude. Better questions produce better answers and, therefore, better results. It effectively steers you toward a happier and more meaningful life.

What do I really want?

How can I be who I want to be?

Why do I do what I do?

If I listen carefully to myself and my body, what do I need right now and how can I give myself exactly that?

What does my inner voice want to tell me?

What would I do if I didn't let fears or doubts hold me back?

What do I find important in life and am I spending enough time on it?

What do I consider essential for a good friendship and does everyone in my inner circle meet this standard?

How can I help myself today?

Can I look at this another way? A way that gives me more peace of mind and confidence?

What does a happy life look like to me and how can I live it more fully now?

What do I consider important to my happiness and how can I give myself that?

What structurally costs me too much energy and how can I distance myself from it or say goodbye to it?

If I want to stay true to myself today, what should I do?

What advice would I give myself if I were my own best friend?

Do I feel free to make my own choices?

How can I be myself more?

What would I do if I knew no one would judge me?

How would I feel if my dreams came true and how can I find that feeling more often in my daily life?

What did I do today that I am proud of?

Where am I growing and how can I continue to grow?

What little moments make me happy and how can I add more of them to my day?

What is not helping me move forward and how am I going to change that?

With what intention do I go about my day?

To stay true to yourself and live life the way you want, it is important to check in with yourself regularly. This way you get the confirmation that you are on the right track or the awareness that it is time to make some changes. The sooner you check in with yourself, the more you can pick up on subtle signals and not drift too far before you take action. It doesn't always have to be big gestures; sometimes it only takes a few small adjustments to make you feel good again. Ask

I haven't changed.
I just became myself more.

yourself deep questions and take the time to really feel and answer them honestly.

The thing that is going to help you the most in life is not the great advice you are given, but the probing questions you are asked that make you think. If you train yourself to ask yourself those questions more often, you will find that the best answers are *within* yourself. You will get to know yourself, be yourself and choose yourself more and more. You will be able to more effectively find your way if you accidentally stray from your path or consciously choose to take a different route. The right questions always help you come home to yourself. And then there comes a day when you wake up, look at your life and the people around you and think, yes, I have really chosen myself. I am myself and I live my life the way I want to.

ACKNOWLEDGEMENTS

My family, thank you for the countless hours of babysitting and allowing me to listen to what you were saying with half an ear because my thoughts were with this book. Thanks to you I have the space to pursue my passion and for that I am very grateful.

My loveliest girls, thank you for all you teach me about myself and life. I want nothing more than for you two to feel free to be your most authentic selves. I hope that in a few years' time you will understand why mommy was so busy writing this book but still love to come and get advice from me personally. My door is forever open.

Binkie, I am glad that staying true to myself has also brought you something good. A few less hikes, because this book had to be finished, but a lot more space to do your own running around because of our choice to live in the middle of the wilderness in Ibiza. From now on back to our daily hikes, promise.

Moniek, thanks to you I can be 100% myself in business and I am grateful for that. We are proof that daring to take big risks, embracing shit and having endless trust in your own inner voice really does lead to those unprecedented heights in the end. Thanks to you, work feels like a hobby that got slightly out of hand.

Team Moonshot Publishing, being who I am, I pushed us all to the limit again during this process. I am thankful that you enthusiastically worked through evenings, nights, and weekends to contribute your expertise to this project and we can be so proud of the results.

And to you. I am grateful you are trusting me to accompany you for a bit on the journey back to yourself. Wherever your choices may take you in this life, let it be a place that is true to yourself that makes you happy.

FURTHER READING

Inspiration for this book came from my college years, from postgraduate courses, from lectures by peers, from my own companies, and from the thousands of people I was fortunate enough to coach, plus all the inspiring life stories I hear every day, directly and indirectly, online and offline.

The following is a list of the main books I consulted:

This is the main literature consulted:

American Psychiatric Association (2013). *Diagnostic and Statistical Manual of Mental Disorders.* American Psychiatric Publishing.

Beck, J.S. (1999). *Cognitieve gedragstherapie: theorie en praktijk (Cognitive behavioral therapy: Theory and practice).* HB Publishers

Beijnen, C. (2024). *De formule: De 6 stappen om je droomleven te manifesteren ("The Formula: The 6 steps to manifesting your dream life").* Moonshot Publishing

Boon, L. (1982). *Geschiedenis van de psychologie ("History of psychology").* Boom

Brown, B. (2015). *Daring greatly: How the courage to be vulnerable transforms the way we live, love, parent, and lead.* Penguin Publishing Group

Cramer, P. (1998). *Coping and defense mechanism: What is the difference?* Journal of personality, 66, 6, 919-935.

Clear, J. (2018). *Atomic habits: An easy & proven way to build good habits and break bad ones.* Random House

Dispenza, J. (2013). *Breaking the habit of being yourself: How to lose your mind and create a new one.* Hay House Inc.

Dyer, W.W. (2001). *You'll see it when you believe it: The way to your personal transformation.* William Morrow Paperbacks

Joseph, S. (2019). *Authentic: How to be yourself and why it matters.* Piatkus

Kabat-Zinn, J. (2013). *Mindfulness voor beginners (Mindfulness for Beginners).* Nieuwezijds BV

Kaufman, S.B., & Jauk, E. (2020). *Healthy selfishness and pathological altruism: Measuring two paradoxical forms of selfishness.* Frontiers in Psychology

Newman, G. E. (2018). *The psychology of authenticity.* Review of General Psychology. 23(1), 8-18.

Obama, M. (2022). *The light we carry: Overcoming in uncertain times.* Crown Publishing

Rogers, C. (1995). *A way of being.* Mariner Books

Tolan, J. (2003). *Skills in person-centred counselling & psychotherapy.* Sage Publications Ltd

Ware, B. (2012). *The top five regrets of the dying: A life transformed by the dearly departing.* Hay House UK

Shazer, S. De & Dolan, Y. (2008). *Oplossingsgerichte therapie in de praktijk: wonderen die werken* (More than miracles: The state of the art of solution-focused brief therapy). Boom

Blum, S., Brow, M. & R.C. Silver (2012). *Encyclopedia of human behavior (Second edition).* Academic Press

ALSO BY THIS AUTHOR

The Power of Choice
How to hack your happiness

Happy Life 365
The art of a joyous mindset

Scan below QR code to learn more.